Kaplan Publishing are constantly finding ways to make a difference to your studies and our exciting online resources really do offer something different to students looking for exam success.

KU-533-998

This book comes with free MyKaplan online resources so that you can study anytime, anywhere. **This free online resource is not sold separately and is included in the price of the book.**

Having purchased this book, you have access to the following online study materials:

CONTENT	AAT	
	Text	Kit
Electronic version of the book	✓	✓
Progress tests with instant answers	✓	
Mock assessments online	✓	✓
Material updates	✓	✓

How to access your online resources

Kaplan Financial students will already have a MyKaplan account and these extra resources will be available to you online. You do not need to register again, as this process was completed when you enrolled. If you are having problems accessing online materials, please ask your course administrator.

If you are not studying with Kaplan and did not purchase your book via a Kaplan website, to unlock your extra online resources please go to www.mykaplan.co.uk/addabook (even if you have set up an account and registered books previously). You will then need to enter the ISBN number (on the title page and back cover) and the unique pass key number contained in the scratch panel below to gain access. You will also be required to enter additional information during this process to set up or confirm your account details.

If you purchased through Kaplan Flexible Learning or via the Kaplan Publishing website you will automatically receive an e-mail invitation to MyKaplan. Please register your details using this email to gain access to your content. If you do not receive the e-mail or book content, please contact Kaplan Publishing.

Your Code and Information

This code can only be used once for the registration of one book online. This registration and your online content will expire when the final sittings for the examinations covered by this book have taken place. Please allow one hour from the time you submit your book details for us to process your request.

Please scratch the film to access your MyKaplan code.

Please be aware that this code is case-sensitive and you will need to include the dashes within the passcode, but not when entering the ISBN. For further technical support, please visit www.MyKaplan.co.uk

NTS

ΓEXT

ımework

AQ2016

This Study Text supports study for the following AAT qualifications:

AAT Advanced Diploma in Accounting – Level 3

AAT Advanced Certificate in Bookkeeping – Level 3

AAT Advanced Diploma in Accounting at SCQF Level 6

British Library Cataloguing-in-Publication Data

A catalogue record for this book is available from the British Library.

Published by
Kaplan Publishing UK
Unit 2, The Business Centre
Molly Millars Lane
Wokingham
Berkshire
RG41 2QZ

ISBN: 978-1-78740-268-3

CONTENTS

INTRODUCTION

HOW TO USE THESE MATERIALS

These Kaplan Publishing learning materials have been carefully designed to make your learning experience as easy as possible and to give you the best chance of success in your AAT assessments.

They contain a number of features to help you in the study process.

The sections on the Unit Guide, the Assessment and Study Skills should be read before you commence your studies.

They are designed to familiarise you with the nature and content of the assessment and to give you tips on how best to approach your studies.

STUDY TEXT

This Study Text has been specially prepared for the revised AAT qualification introduced in September 2016.

It is written in a practical and interactive style:

- Key terms and concepts are clearly defined.

- All topics are illustrated with practical examples with clearly worked solutions based on sample tasks provided by the AAT in the new examining style.

- Frequent practice activities throughout the chapters ensure that what you have learnt is regularly reinforced.

- 'Test your understanding' activities are included within each chapter to apply your learning and develop your understanding.

ICON

The study chapters include the following icons throughout.

They are designed to assist you in your studies by identifying key definitions and the points at which you can test yourself on the knowledge gained.

 Definition

These sections explain important areas of knowledge which must be understood and reproduced in an assessment.

 Example

The illustrative examples can be used to help develop an understanding of topics before attempting the activity exercises.

 Test your understanding

These are exercises which give the opportunity to assess your understanding of all the assessment areas.

Quality and accuracy are of the utmost importance to us so if you spot an error in any of our products, please send an email to mykaplanreporting@kaplan.com with full details.

Our Quality Co-ordinator will work with our technical team to verify the error and take action to ensure it is corrected in future editions.

KAPLAN PUBLISHING

UNIT GUIDE

Ethics for Accountants is a Level 3 mandatory unit that is examined as part of the synoptic assessment.

Purpose of the unit

This unit is about professional ethics in an accounting environment. It seeks to ensure that students have an excellent understanding of why accountants need to act ethically, of the principles of ethical working, of what is meant by ethical behaviour at work, and of when and how to take action in relation to unethical behaviour and illegal acts.

This unit supports students in:

- working within the ethical code applicable to accountants and accounting technicians

- ensuring the public has a good level of confidence in accounting practices or functions

- protecting their own and their organisation's professional reputation and legal liability

- upholding principles of sustainability.

Students will learn the core aspects of the ethical code for accountants, as it relates to their work as accounting technicians and as exemplified in AAT's Code of Professional Ethics. They will understand the ethical principles of integrity, objectivity, professional competence and due care, professional behaviour and confidentiality, and will learn to apply these principles to analyse and judge ethical situations at work.

They will also understand that acting ethically derives from core personal and organisational values, such as honesty, transparency and fairness, as well as from professional ethics. Understanding the conceptual framework of principles, threats and safeguards contained in the ethical code, plus its process for ethical conflict resolution, will enable students to apply a systematic approach to ethical problems that they may encounter.

Students will, therefore, develop skills in analysing problems, and in judging between 'right' and 'wrong' behaviour in a given context. They will also be able to identify alternative courses of action to resolve an ethical problem, and select the most appropriate action in the circumstances.

Money laundering regulations mean that accountants can be exposed to legal liability for keeping quiet in certain circumstances, or for telling the wrong person about suspected wrongdoing. Students will learn when and how the money laundering regulations apply, and their responsibilities in respect of them. They will also learn about reporting to the authorities in respect of suspected money laundering. In certain other circumstances, it may be appropriate for an accountant to report, 'speak up' or blow the whistle on unethical behaviour.

Finally, students will understand the basis and nature of the accountant's ethical responsibilities to uphold sustainability in their organisation.

Ethics for Accountants is a mandatory unit. It links with Work Effectively in Finance at Level 2, and with Accounting Systems and Controls at Level 4. There are opportunities to include aspects of acting ethically at work when delivering the other mandatory units at Level 3.

Ethics for Accountants is a **mandatory unit** in this qualification.

Learning outcomes

On completion of this unit the learner will be able to:

- understand the need to act ethically
- understand the relevance to the accountant's work of the ethical code for professional accountants
- recognise how to act ethically in an accounting role
- identify action to take in relation to unethical behaviour or illegal acts.

Scope of content

To perform this unit effectively you will need to know and understand the following:

Chapter

1 Understand the need to act ethically

1.1 Explain why it is important to act ethically

Students need to know:

• that the accountant acting ethically: supports the level of confidence that the public has in accountants, enhances the organisation's probity and reputation, enhances the accountant's own professional reputation, protects the accountant's legal liability	Throughout
• that it is important for an accountant to comply with the ethical code and act ethically at all times	Throughout
• that the accountant has a public interest duty to society as well as to the client or employer	2
• that maintenance of the reputation of accountancy as a profession is one of the objectives of the ethical code	1, 5
• that the accountant's compliance with the ethical code is a professional not a legal obligation	1, 2
• that members of professional accountancy bodies are held to account by those bodies for breaches of their ethical codes	2, 3
• when disciplinary action by the relevant professional accountancy body may be brought against the accountant for misconduct, and the possible penalties that can arise	2, 3
• that internal disciplinary procedures may be brought against the accountant by the employer for unethical or illegal behaviour	2
• that organisations may suffer fines or reputational damage as a result of unethical behaviour and non-compliance with values, codes and regulations.	3

Chapter

1.2 Explain how to act ethically

Students need to know:

- that specific action may have to be taken in order to behave ethically: ignoring a problem, or doing nothing about it, may not be ethical   2

- that simply complying with regulations may not constitute ethical behaviour, depending on the circumstances   5

- that a methodical approach to resolving ethical problems is advisable   1

- that the ethical code takes a principles-based not a rules-based approach to ethics, conduct and practice.   1

1.3 Explain the importance of values, culture and codes of practice/conduct

Students need to know:

- that an organisation's values, corporate culture and leadership govern its decisions and actions   2

- that conflict may arise and have to be resolved between an individual's key personal values and organisational values   1, 5

- the importance to an organisation of: an ethics-based culture that discourages unethical or illegal practices, an ethical 'tone at the top'/leadership   1, 5

- that codes of conduct, codes of practice and regulations may affect ethical decisions by organisations and individuals.   3

Chapter

2   Understand the relevance to the accountant's work of the ethical code for professional accountants

2.1   Explain the ethical code's conceptual framework of principles, threats, safeguards and professional judgement

Students need to know:

• that an accountant should evaluate threats to compliance with the fundamental principles then implement safeguards, using professional judgement, that eliminate the threats or reduce them to an acceptable level	1, 2, 3
• the types of threat to the fundamental principles	1, 5
• the types of safeguard that may be applied	1, 5
• that documented organisational policies on various issues can be used as safeguards to prevent threats and ethical conflict from arising	1, 3
• what an accountant should do when a threat cannot be eliminated or reduced to an acceptable level.	1

2.2   Explain the importance of acting with integrity

Students need to know:

• the meaning of integrity from the ethical code	1
• the effect of accountants being associated with misleading information	1
• what is meant by the key ethical values of honesty, transparency and fairness	1
• that it is important to act at all times with integrity, honesty, transparency and fairness when liaising with clients, suppliers and colleagues	1, 2
• that integrity is threatened in particular by self-interest and familiarity threats.	1

Chapter

2.3 Explain the importance of objectivity

Students need to know:

- the meaning of objectivity from the ethical code — 1

- the importance of maintaining a professional distance between professional duties and personal life at all times — 1, 5

- what is meant by a conflict of interest, including self-interest threats arising from financial interests, compensation and incentives linked to financial reporting and decision making — 1, 5

- the importance of appearing to be objective as well as actually being objective — 1

- the importance of professional scepticism when exercising professional judgement — 1

- how accountants may deal with offers of gifts and hospitality — 1

- that gifts and hospitality may pose threats to objectivity as inducements — 4

- that compromised objectivity may lead to accusations of bribery or fraud — 4

- that objectivity is threatened in particular by intimidation, self-review and advocacy threats as well as by self-interest and familiarity threats. — 1, 4

2.4 Explain the importance of behaving professionally

Students need to know:

- the meaning of professional behaviour from the ethical code — 1

- that the ethical code as a whole sets out the required standards of behaviour for accountants and how to achieve them — 1

- that compliance with relevant laws and regulations is a minimum requirement, so an act that is permitted by the law/regulations is not necessarily ethical — 1, 2, 4

Chapter

- that bringing disrepute on the profession may in itself lead to disciplinary action by a professional accountancy body — 1, 2

- that professional behaviour is threatened in particular by self-interest, self-review and familiarity threats. — 1

2.5   Explain the importance of being competent and acting with due care

Students need to know:

- the meaning of professional competence and of due care from the ethical code — 1

- that due care and diligence mean acting in accordance with the requirements of a task: carefully, thoroughly and on a timely basis — 1

- that professional qualifications and continuing professional development (CPD) support professional competence — 2

- the areas in which up-to-date technical knowledge for an accountant's competence may be critical — 2

- the consequences of an accountant failing to work competently and with due care: breach of contract in the supply of services; professional negligence; accusations of fraud or money laundering — 2, 4

- that professional competence and due care are threatened in particular by self-interest, self-review and familiarity threats. — 1

2.6   Explain the importance of confidentiality and when confidential information may be disclosed

Students need to know:

- the meaning of confidentiality from the ethical code — 1

- the types of situation that present threats to confidentiality — 1

- that an accountant may on occasion be justified in disclosing confidential information — 1

	Chapter

- when it may be appropriate to disclose confidential information, and when it must be disclosed — 1

- to whom a disclosure of confidential information may be made — 1

- that information confidentiality may be affected by compliance with data protection laws as well as by the ethical principle — 1, 4

- that confidentiality is threatened in particular by self-interest, intimidation and familiarity threats. — 1

2.7 Explain the stages in the ethical code's process for ethical conflict resolution

Students need to know:

- how ethical conflict situations could arise in a work context — 1

- the stages in the process for ethical conflict resolution when a situation presents a conflict in application of the fundamental principles — 1

- that documented organisational policies on various issues can be used as safeguards to prevent ethical conflict from arising. — 1

3 Recognise how to act ethically in an accounting role

3.1 Distinguish between ethical and unethical behaviour

Students need to be able to:

- apply values and principles to identify whether behaviour is ethical or unethical in a given situation — 1

- apply key organisational values to a given situation, including complying with regulations in spirit as well as letter, with regard to: being transparent with customers and suppliers; reporting financial and regulatory information clearly and on time; whether to accept and give gifts and hospitality; paying suppliers a fair price and on time; providing fair treatment, decent wages and good working conditions to employees; using social media — 1, 2, 5

Chapter

- identify situations where there is pressure to behave unethically, especially from self-interest, familiarity and intimidation threats to the fundamental principles.   1

3.2 Analyse a situation using the conceptual framework and the conflict resolution process

Students need to be able to:

- apply the conceptual framework to a situation   1

- apply the conflict resolution process to a situation   1

- decide what to do if the conflict resolution process does not resolve the problem (take advice externally)   1, 2, 3, 5

- decide what to do if the conflict cannot be resolved (refuse to remain associated with the matter creating the conflict, or resign).   1

3.3 Develop an ethical course of action

Students need to be able to:

- formulate a specific course of action to address the ethical concerns that have arisen   1

- decide when and how advice about an ethical dilemma or unethical behaviour with regard to their own work, clients, suppliers or colleagues should be sought from a colleague or manager, or from the helpline of the employer or professional body   1, 2, 3, 5

- refer instances of unethical behaviour to responsible persons at work, by reference initially to line management, using discretion and maintaining confidentiality.   1, 5

Chapter

3.4 **Justify an appropriate action when requested to perform tasks that are beyond current experience or expertise**

Students need to be able to:

• recognise in a given situation that an accountant has been asked to complete work for which they do not have sufficient expertise, information, time, training or resources	5
• decide the appropriate time at which advice about such concerns should be sought	5
• decide what to do in such a situation.	5

3.5 **Explain the ethical responsibilities of accountants in upholding the principles of sustainability**

Students need to know:

• that sustainability means taking a long-term view and allowing the needs of present generations to be met, without compromising the ability of future generations to meet their own needs	6
• that sustainability requires the organisation to consider the needs of its wider stakeholders	6
• that the accountant's ethical duty of integrity includes being transparent and producing information that is not misleading, which together support sustainability	1, 6
• that accountants have a public interest duty to protect society as a whole so should promote:	1, 6
– social and environmental as well as economic/financial aspects when measuring an organisation's income, expenses, assets and liabilities, and when assisting with decision making	6
– the long-term responsible management and use of resources by their organisation	6
– the running of their organisation in a sustainable manner in relation to products and services, customers, employees, the workplace, the supply chain and business functions and processes.	6

KAPLAN PUBLISHING

Chapter

4   Identify action to take in relation to unethical behaviour or illegal acts

4.1   Analyse a given situation in light of money laundering law and regulations

Students need to know:

- the possible offences under money laundering law and regulations, and their consequences for accountants and for organisations   3

- the events that may occur in relation to the accountant, colleagues, the organisation, its customers and its suppliers that give rise to obligations for the accountant under money laundering law and regulations   3

- the consequences for an accountant of failing to act appropriately in response to such events, including the potential for the offences of 'tipping off' and 'failure to disclose'   3

- the consequences for any person of 'prejudicing an investigation'   3

- the nature of the protection given to accountants by protected disclosures and authorised disclosures under the money laundering law and regulations   3

- the position specifically of accountants employed in a business regarding external reporting of the employer's suspected illegal activities under money laundering law and regulations, when the accountant is directly involved, and also when they are not directly involved.   3

Chapter

4.2 Identify the relevant body to which questionable behaviour must be reported

Students need to know:

- the nature and role of relevant external authorities in relation to accountants and the money laundering regulations — 3

- the relevant authority or internal department to which reports about money laundering should be made — 3

- when and to whom tax errors should be reported — 3

- the relevant external authorities to which reports about other forms of illegal activity may be made — 3

- that there may be a prescribed internal department and/or external professional body/agency to which reports may be made regarding unethical behaviour and breaches of confidentiality. — 3, 4

4.3 Report suspected money laundering in accordance with the regulations

Students need to be able to:

- select the information that should be reported by an accountant making a required disclosure in either an internal report or a suspicious activity report (SAR) regarding suspicions about money laundering — 3

- identify when the required disclosure should be made. — 3, 5

KAPLAN PUBLISHING

Chapter

4.4   Decide when and how to report unethical behaviour by employers, colleagues or clients/customers

Students need to be able to:

- identify when it is appropriate to report that a breach of the ethical code has taken place   3

- report in line with formal internal whistle-blowing or 'speak-out' procedures that may be available for reporting unethical behaviour   3

- seek advice confidentially from relevant helplines as appropriate   3

- identify circumstances when there may be public interest disclosure protection available under statute for blowing the whistle externally in the public interest in relation to certain illegal or unethical acts by the employer   3

- seek third-party advice before blowing the whistle externally, since the legal protection available to an external whistle-blower is limited.   3

UNIT LINK TO THE SYNOPTIC ASSESSMENT THE ASSESSMENT

AAT AQ16 introduced a Synoptic Assessment, which students must complete if they are to achieve the appropriate qualification upon completion of a qualification. In the case of the Advanced Diploma in Accounting, students must pass all of the mandatory assessments and the Synoptic Assessment to achieve the qualification.

As a Synoptic Assessment is attempted following completion of individual units, it draws upon knowledge and understanding from those units. It may be appropriate for students to retain their study materials for individual units until they have successfully completed the Synoptic Assessment for that qualification.

This unit is solely assessed within the Synoptic assessment so all learning objectives are relevant.

Test specification for this unit assessment

Assessment type	Marking type	Duration of exam
Computer-based synoptic assessment	Partially computer/ partially human marked	2 hours 45 minutes, composed of two components (plus an additional 15 minutes to upload evidence)

Assessment objective	Weighting
A01 Demonstrate an understanding of the relevance of the ethical code for accountants, the need to act ethically in a given situation, and the appropriate action to take in reporting questionable behaviour	15%
A02 Prepare accounting records and respond to errors, omissions and other concerns, in accordance with accounting and ethical principles and relevant regulations	15%

KAPLAN PUBLISHING

A03	
Apply ethical and accounting principles when preparing final accounts for different types of organisation, develop ethical courses of action and communicate relevant information effectively	15%
A04	
Use relevant spreadsheet skills to analyse, interpret and report management accounting data	25%
A05	
Prepare financial accounting information, comprising extended trial balances and final accounts for sole traders and partnerships, using spreadsheets	30%
Total	**100%**

NB Of the above, AO1; AO2 and AO3 specifically relate to EFTA but will form part of the overall assessment.

STUDY SKILLS

Preparing to study

Devise a study plan

Determine which times of the week you will study.

Split these times into sessions of at least one hour for study of new material. Any shorter periods could be used for revision or practice.

Put the times you plan to study onto a study plan for the weeks from now until the assessment and set yourself targets for each period of study – in your sessions make sure you cover the whole course, activities and the associated questions in the workbook at the back of the manual.

If you are studying more than one unit at a time, try to vary your subjects as this can help to keep you interested and to see the relationships between different subjects.

When working through your course, compare your progress with your plan and, if necessary, re-plan your work (perhaps including extra sessions) or, if you are ahead, do some extra revision/practice questions.

Effective studying

Active reading

You are not expected to learn the text by rote, rather, you must understand what you are reading and be able to use it to pass the assessment and develop good practice.

A good technique is to use SQ3Rs – Survey, Question, Read, Recall, and Review:

1 **Survey the chapter**

   Look at the headings and read the introduction, knowledge, skills and content, so as to get an overview of what the chapter deals with.

2 **Question**

   Whilst undertaking the survey ask yourself the questions you hope the chapter will answer for you.

3 **Read**

   Read through the chapter thoroughly working through the activities.

4   Recall

At the end of each section and at the end of the chapter, try to recall the main ideas of the section / chapter without referring to the text. This is best done after short break of a couple of minutes after the reading stage.

5   Review

Check that your recall notes are correct.

You may also find it helpful to re-read the chapter to try and see the topic(s) it deals with as a whole.

Note taking

Taking notes is a useful way of learning, but do not simply copy out the text.

The notes must:

- be in your own words
- be concise
- cover the key points
- be well organised
- be modified as you study further chapters in this text or in related ones.

Trying to summarise a chapter without referring to the text can be a useful way of determining which areas you know and which you don't.

Three ways of taking notes

1   Summarise the key points of a chapter

2   Make linear notes

A list of headings, subdivided with sub-headings listing the key points.

If you use linear notes, you can use different colours to highlight key points and keep topic areas together.

Use plenty of space to make your notes easy to use.

3 **Try a diagrammatic form**

The most common of which is a mind map.

To make a mind map, put the main heading in the centre of the paper and put a circle around it.

Draw lines radiating from this to the main sub-headings which again have circles around them.

Continue the process from the sub-headings to sub-sub-headings.

Highlighting and underlining

You may also find it useful to underline or highlight key points in your study text – but do be selective.

You may also wish to make notes in the margins.

Revision phase

Kaplan has produced material specifically designed for your final examination preparation for this unit.

These include pocket revision notes and a bank of revision questions ('revision kit') specifically in the style of the new syllabus.

Further guidance on how to approach the final stage of your studies is given in the revision kit.

Further reading

In addition to this text, you should also read the 'Student section' of the 'Accounting Technician' magazine every month to keep abreast of any guidance from the examiners.

KAPLAN PUBLISHING

Ethics – The principles

1

Introduction

In this chapter we look at the fundamental principles of integrity, objectivity, professional and technical competence, due care, confidentiality and professional behaviour.

These underpin the whole syllabus so it is vital that you know, understand and can apply the principles.

The Ethics for Accountants syllabus does **not** require you to have a detailed knowledge of the AAT Code of Ethics and other AAT regulations. However, you are expected to know the key aspects of the underpinning IFAC Code of Ethics for Professional Accountants:

- The purpose of the code.

- The fundamental principles and the conceptual framework.

ASSESSMENT CRITERIA

1.1 Explain why it is important to act ethically
1.2 Explain how to act ethically
1.3 Explain the importance of values, culture and codes of practice/conduct
2.1 Explain the ethical code's conceptual framework of principles, threats, safeguards and professional judgement
2.2 Explain the importance of acting with integrity
2.3 Explain the importance of objectivity
2.4 Explain the importance of behaving professionally
2.5 Explain the importance of being competent and acting with due care
2.6 Explain the importance of confidentiality and when confidential information may be disclosed
2.7 Explain the stages in the ethical code's process for ethical conflict resolution
3.1 Distinguish between ethical and unethical behaviour
3.2 Analyse a situation using the conceptual framework and the conflict resolution process
3.3 Develop an ethical course of action
3.5 Explain the ethical responsibilities of accountants in upholding the principles of sustainability.

CONTENTS

1 Introduction to business ethics

2 Fundamental principles

3 Threats and safeguards

4 Dealing with ethical conflicts

1 Introduction to business ethics

1.1 What do we mean by 'ethics'?

> 🔍 **Definition – Ethics**
>
> Ethics can be defined as the "moral principles that govern a person's behaviour or the conducting of an activity".
>
> *The Oxford English Dictionary*

Ethics is thus concerned with how one should act in a certain situation, about 'doing the right thing' and is ultimately about morality – the difference between right and wrong.

> 💡 **Example 1 – Ethical choices**
>
> Consider the following ethical dilemmas:
>
> - You buy something in a shop and later discover that they have under-charged you for an item. Do you go back and tell them?
>
> - You want a new designer label tee-shirt but think it is too expensive. Would you buy a cheap fake copy if you saw one for sale while on holiday?
>
> - Have you ever told your employer that you were sick when the truth was you simply wanted a day off?
>
> - Would you stop buying a particular product if you found out that the working conditions in the factories where they are made were far below UK standards (e.g. concerning hours worked, pay rates, sickness policy, discrimination, use of child labour, etc)?
>
> - Have you ever 'exaggerated' an expense claim?
>
> Does the fact that you are a (student) member of a professional body affect your answers?

1.2 Business ethics

Business ethics is the application of ethical principles to the problems typically encountered in a business setting.

There is no separate 'business ethic' that puts it beyond the range of normal moral judgements.

> ### 💡 Example 2 – Typical issues in business ethics
>
> Some typical issues addressed in business ethics include:
>
> - 'creative accounting' to misrepresent financial performance
> - misleading advertising
> - aggressive personal selling (e.g. insurance or double glazing)
> - unfair terms in contracts (e.g. cancelling a gym membership)
> - data protection and privacy
> - the difference between corporate hospitality and bribery
> - the difference between business intelligence and industrial espionage
> - political contributions to gain influence
> - corporate governance
> - corporate crime, including insider trading and price fixing
> - employee issues, such as discrimination or unfair dismissal
> - whistleblowing
> - environmental issues and related social concerns
> - marketing, sales and negotiation techniques
> - product issues such as patent and copyright infringement, planned obsolescence, product liability and product defects
> - using legal loopholes to avoid paying tax.

When ethical values get distorted or compromised, the impact can be enormous. Ethics and ethical standards have thus become the focus of greater attention by organisations, especially in the area of reputation management. Greater emphasis is now placed on accountability, ethics, codes of conduct and monitoring and reporting of violations.

1.3 Ethical influences

Each of us has our own set of values and beliefs that we have evolved over the course of our lives through our education, experiences and upbringing. We all have our own ideas of what is right and what is wrong and these ideas can vary between individuals and cultures.

There are a number of factors that affect ethical obligations.

(i) **The law**

For example, deceptive advertising is illegal and violators of this law are liable to large fines, court action and/or loss of goodwill.

Legislation hopefully makes it very clear what is acceptable as a minimum standard. However, ethics is more than just obeying the law.

For example, using legal loopholes to minimise a global firm's tax bill may not be illegal but is increasingly viewed as unethical.

(ii) **Government regulations**

For example, regulations set standards on issues such as unfair competition, unsafe products, etc. Failure to comply with these regulations could lead to criminal charges, or fines etc.

Unfortunately, some firms will still find ways to get round such regulations.

Example 3 – Artificial sweeteners

In 1970 cyclamates (a type of artificial sweetener) were banned in the USA following evidence that they were carcinogenic.

Following the ban a major US food manufacturer still sold 300,000 cases of cyclamate sweetened food overseas instead.

(iii) **Ethical codes**

Many organisations have codes that clearly state the ethical standards and principles an employee or member should follow.

For example, as an AAT student you are expected to follow the AAT Code of Professional Ethics.

Generally, written codes clarify the ethical issues and principles but leave the resolution to the individual's conscience.

Ethical codes are usually followed if written down and enforced – say by disciplinary procedures. However, many companies have 'unwritten' codes of practice and/or have no method of enforcement.

(iv) **Social pressure**

Many people draw their values from what they see other people doing, whether on the news or people they know. However, social pressure can change, just as society changes.

For example, many politicians comment on a decline in family values in the UK.

Many protest groups and activists hope to change public values with the long term hope that new values become reflected in law. A good example of this is the change in discrimination legislation over the last hundred years.

(v)   Corporate culture

 Definition – Corporate culture

Corporate culture is defined as "the sum total of all the beliefs, attitudes, norms and customs that prevail within an organisation" or "the way we do things around here".

Ideally we want a culture that supports and encourages ethical behaviour.

For example, if everyone else is exaggerating expense claims or covering up mistakes, then this can quickly become a norm of behaviour that new employees soon adopt.

Of particular importance is the example set by senior management – sometimes referred to as the 'tone at the top'.

It is important to note that there can often be tension between personal standards and the goals of the organisation.

Suppose you work for a company selling banned substances overseas. It is not illegal, but it may be against your personal values to sell these products to unsuspecting overseas clients. What would you do if this action were a direct order from a superior? Does this take away your responsibility?

1.4   The costs and benefits of business ethics

It can be argued that the primary purpose of a business is to try and earn a profit. In a company, for instance, the directors have been employed in order to earn the owners of the business a return on their investment.

Some have concluded from this that going beyond the **legal** minimum standard of behaviour is contrary to the directors' duty to make money and that behaving ethically increases costs and reduces profits.

For example:

- Increased cost of sourcing materials from ethical sources (e.g. Fairtrade products or free range eggs).

- Having to turn away business from customers considered to be unethical (e.g. an 'ethical' bank may choose not to invest in a company that manufactures weapons).

- The management time that can be taken up by planning and implementation of ethical practices.

However, as well as the moral argument to act ethically, there can be commercial benefits to firms from acting ethically:

- Having good ethics can attract customers.

  This can be because good ethics tend to enhance a company's reputation and therefore its brand. Given the choice, many customers will prefer to trade with a company they feel is ethical.

- Good ethics can result in a more effective workforce.

  A reputation for good business ethics is likely to involve good working conditions for employees, allowing the business to attract a higher calibre of staff.

  Avoiding discrimination against workers is likely to give the company access to a wider human resource base.

- Ethics programmes can cultivate strong teamwork and improve productivity.

- Ethics can give cost savings.

  Avoiding pollution will tend to save companies in the long run – many governments are now fining or increasing taxes of more polluting businesses.

- Ethics can reduce risk.

  Many firms have failed due to unethical practices within them.

 Example 4 – Enron

Enron, a major US energy company, filed for bankruptcy in 2001. Among the many reasons for its failure were dubious accounting practices (for example, in how they recognised revenue), poor corporate governance and failure by their external auditors, Arthur Andersen.

There were even attempts to hide the problems, with workers being told to destroy all audit material, except for the most basic work papers.

1.5   The Institute of Business Ethics – Simple test

According to the Institute of Business Ethics, a simple ethical test for a business decision could be reached in answering the following three questions:

Question	Explanation
Transparency	Do I mind others knowing what I have decided?
Effect	Does my decision affect or hurt anyone?
Fairness	Would my decision be considered fair by those affected?

2   Fundamental principles

2.1   The Code of Ethics for Professional Accountants

The Code of Ethics for Professional Accountants, published by The International Federation of Accountants (IFAC), forms the basis for the ethical codes of many accountancy bodies, including the AAT, ICAEW, ACCA and CIMA.

The code adopts a principles-based approach. It does not attempt to cover every situation where a member may encounter professional ethical issues, prescribing the way in which he or she should respond. Instead, it adopts a value system, focusing on fundamental professional and ethical principles which are at the heart of proper professional behaviour.

The five key principles are as follows:

(a)   **Integrity**

(b)   **Objectivity**

(c)   **Professional competence and due care**

(d)   **Confidentiality**

(e)   **Professional behaviour**

These are discussed in more detail below.

2.2 A conceptual framework

Professional accountants may face a range of specific threats to compliance with the fundamental principles.

It is impossible to define every situation that creates such threats and specify the appropriate action. In addition, the nature of engagements and work assignments may differ and consequently different threats may exist, requiring the application of different safeguards.

A conceptual framework requires a member to identify, evaluate and address threats to compliance with the fundamental principles, rather than merely comply with a set of specific rules which may be arbitrary.

It also requires that if identified threats are not clearly insignificant, a member shall, where appropriate, apply adequate safeguards to eliminate the threats or reduce them to an acceptable level, so that compliance with the fundamental principles is not compromised.

2.3 Compliance with ethical codes

A professional accountant's responsibility is not just to satisfy the needs of an individual client or employer. It should also be to act in the public interest.

In acting in the public interest a professional accountant should observe and comply with the fundamental ethical requirements shown in the IFAC Code.

AAT members should note that disciplinary action may be taken for non-compliance with the AAT code where the member's conduct is considered to prejudice their status as a member or to reflect adversely on the reputation of AAT. For the purposes of this paper, you do not need to be concerned with the differences between the IFAC code and the AAT code.

Where professional accountants are members of more than one professional body, there may be differences in some areas between the professional and ethical conduct requirements of the different bodies. Where there are differences, members should follow the more stringent provision.

Unethical and dishonest behaviour (and its legal consequences) creates powerful negative public relations within the profession, the wider community and the organisation itself.

2.4 Integrity

 Definition – Integrity

Integrity means that a member must be straightforward and honest in all professional and business relationships. Integrity also implies fair dealing and truthfulness.

Accountants are expected to present financial information fully, honestly and professionally and so that it will be understood in its context.

 Example 5 – Integrity

A professional accountant should not be associated with reports where the information:

- contains a materially false or misleading statement

- contains statements or information furnished recklessly

- has omissions that make it misleading.

Accountants should abide by relevant law and regulations and remember that, as well as legal documents, letters and verbal agreements may constitute a binding arrangement.

Accountants should strive to be fair and socially responsible and respect cultural differences when dealing with overseas colleagues or contacts. Promises may not be legally binding but repeatedly going back on them can destroy trust, break relationships and lose co-operation.

To maintain integrity, members have the following responsibilities:

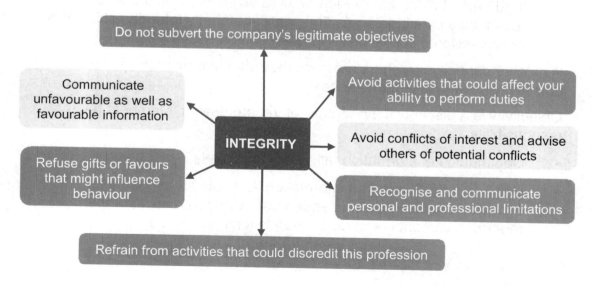

2.5 Objectivity

 Definition – Objectivity

Objectivity means that a member must not allow bias, conflict of interest or undue influence of others to override professional or business judgements.

 Example 6 – Objectivity

Suppose you are part of the audit team at a major client:

- If you also own shares in the client company, then this could be viewed as a conflict of interest.

- If you receive excessive hospitality and discounts from the client then this could be seen as an attempt to influence (bribe?) you and compromise your objectivity.

Objectivity can also be defined as 'the state of mind which has regard to all considerations relevant to the task in hand but no other.' It is closely linked to the concept of independence:

- **Independence of mind** is the state of mind that permits the provision of an opinion without being affected by influences that compromise professional judgement, allowing an individual to act with integrity and exercise objectivity and professional scepticism.

- **Independence of appearance** is the avoidance of facts and circumstances that are so significant that a reasonable and informed third party, having knowledge of all relevant information, would reasonably conclude that a firm's or a member's integrity, objectivity or professional scepticism had been compromised.

Whatever capacity members serve in, they should demonstrate their objectivity in varying circumstances.

Objectivity is a distinguishing feature of the profession. Members have a responsibility to:

- Communicate information fairly and objectively.

- Disclose fully all relevant information that could reasonably be expected to influence an intended user's understanding of the reports, comments, and recommendations presented.

2.6 Professional competence and due care

Definition – Professional competence

Professional competence means that a member has a continuing duty to maintain professional knowledge and skill at the level required to ensure that a client or employer receives competent professional service based on current developments in practice, legislation and techniques.

Definition – Due care

Due care means a member must act diligently and in accordance with applicable technical and professional standards when providing professional services.

In agreeing to provide professional services, a professional accountant implies that there is a level of competence necessary to perform those services and that his or her knowledge, skill and experience will be applied with reasonable care and diligence.

Example 7 – Professional competence

Suppose you are an accountant in practice. A new client asks you to perform their tax computations but it would involve aspects of inheritance tax that you have not looked at for many years.

Unless you have other people with the required tax expertise in the practice, you should decline the tax work as you are not competent to do it.

Professional accountants must therefore refrain from performing any services that they are not competent to carry out unless appropriate advice and assistance is obtained to ensure that the services are performed satisfactorily.

Professional competence may be divided into two separate phases:

1   Gaining professional competence – for example, by training to gain the AAT qualification.

2   Maintaining professional competence – accountants need to keep up to date with developments in the accountancy profession including relevant national and international pronouncements on accounting, auditing and other relevant regulations and statutory requirements.

Members have a responsibility to:

- Maintain an appropriate level of professional competence by ongoing development of their knowledge and skills.

- Maintain technical and ethical standards in areas relevant to their work through continuing professional development.

- Perform their professional duties in accordance with relevant laws, regulations, and technical standards.

- Prepare complete and clear reports and recommendations after appropriate analysis of relevant and reliable information.

Members should adopt review procedures that will ensure the quality of their professional work is consistent with national and international pronouncements that are issued from time to time.

Due professional care applies to the exercise of professional judgement in the conduct of work performed and implies that the professional approaches matters requiring professional judgement with proper diligence.

Keeping knowledge up to date is covered in more detail in Chapter 2.

2.7 Confidentiality

 Definition – Confidentiality

A member must, in accordance with the law, respect the confidentiality of information acquired as a result of professional and business relationships and not disclose any such information to third parties without proper and specific authority unless there is a legal or professional right or duty to disclose.

Confidential information acquired as a result of professional and business relationships must not be used for the personal advantage of the member or third parties.

Note that confidentiality is not only a matter of disclosure of information – it also concerns using information for personal advantage or for the advantage of a third party.

Example 8 – Confidentiality

Suppose you are an accountant in practice and you discover that the client has just won a major contract. This has yet to be publicised but when a press release is made, then the share price will go up significantly.

If you then buy the (undervalued) shares, then you have breached the principle of confidentiality – not because you told someone but because you used confidential information with the expectation of making a personal gain.

Members should:

- be prudent in the use and protection of information acquired in the course of their duties. (Please note that the duty of confidentiality continues even after the end of the relationship between the member and the employer or client.)

- not use information for any personal gain or in any manner that would be contrary to the law or detrimental to the legitimate and ethical objectives of the organisation.

- inform subordinates as appropriate regarding the confidentiality of information acquired in the course of their work and monitor their activities to assure the maintenance of that confidentiality.

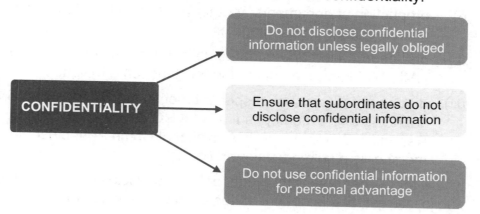

A member must take care to maintain confidentiality even in a social environment. The member should be alert to the possibility of inadvertent disclosure, particularly in circumstances involving close or personal relations, associates and long established business relationships.

Test your understanding 1

You visit a client who is a dealer in sports cars. He sells one of his cars to a customer for £16,000; however he later tells you that the car has a faulty braking system.

What should you do?

- Nothing.

- Tell the customer.

- Tell the client you believe he acted unethically, but that you are bound by confidentiality therefore cannot tell anyone.

- Report your client to the authorities.

The problem with confidentiality is that there are times when disclosure may be permitted or even mandatory.

The following are circumstances where members are or may be required to disclose confidential information or when such disclosure may be appropriate:

(a)   where disclosure is permitted by law and is authorised by the client or the employer

(b)   where disclosure is required by law, for example:

   (i)   production of documents or other provision of evidence in the course of legal proceedings or

   (ii)   disclosure to the appropriate public authorities (for example, HMRC) of infringements of the law that come to light or

   (iii)   disclosure of actual or suspected money laundering or terrorist financing to the member's firm's MLRO (Money Laundering Reporting Officer) or to NCA (National Crime Agency) if the member is a sole practitioner, or

(c)   where there is a professional duty or right to disclose, which is in the public interest, and is not prohibited by law. Examples may include:

   (i)   to comply with the quality review of an IFAC member body or other relevant professional body

   (ii)   to respond to an inquiry or investigation by the AAT or a relevant regulatory or professional body

   (iii)   where it is necessary to protect the member's professional interests in legal proceedings or

   (iv)   to comply with technical standards and ethics requirements.

In deciding whether to disclose confidential information, members should consider the following points:

- whether the interests of all parties, including third parties, could be harmed even though the client or employer (or other person to whom there is a duty of confidentiality) consents to the disclosure of information by the member

- whether all the relevant information is known and substantiated, to the extent that this is practicable. When the situation involves unsubstantiated facts, incomplete information or unsubstantiated conclusions, professional judgement should be used in determining the type of disclosure to be made, if any

- the type of communication or disclosure that may be made and by whom it is to be received; in particular, members should be satisfied that the parties to whom the communication is addressed are appropriate recipients.

2.8   Professional behaviour

 Definition – Professional behaviour

A professional accountant should comply with relevant laws and regulations and should avoid any action that discredits the profession.

A profession is distinguished by certain characteristics including:

- mastery of a particular intellectual skill, acquired by training and education

- adherence by its members to a common code of values and conduct established by its administrating body, including maintaining an outlook which is essentially objective; and

- acceptance of a duty to society as a whole (usually in return for restrictions in use of a title or in the granting of a qualification).

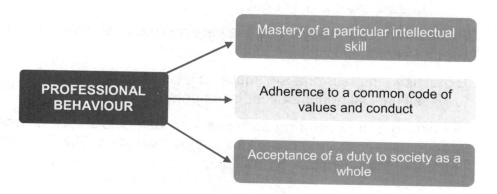

The objectives of the accountancy profession are to work to the highest standards of professionalism, to attain the highest levels of performance and generally to meet the public interest requirement. These objectives require four basic needs to be met:

(i)   **Credibility** – there is a need for credibility in information and information systems.

(ii) **Professionalism** – there is a need to be clearly identified by employers, clients and other interested parties as a professional person in the accountancy field.

(iii) **Quality of services** – assurance is needed that all services obtained from a professional accountant are carried out to the highest standards of performance.

(iv) **Confidence** – users of the services of professional accountants should be able to feel confident that there is a framework of professional ethics to govern the provision of services.

The most important privilege conferred on professionals is the right to a 'professional opinion'. Professionals can be distinguished from others in society by their right to form an opinion and to base their services and/or products on this opinion. Misuse of this privilege can result in serious harm, thus it is only granted to those who are able to show by education and experience the ability to properly exercise this right.

What is understood by the term 'professionalism' will depend on the context and culture of the organisation.

It should include:

- **Professional/client relationship:**
    - the client presumes his or her needs will be met without having to direct the process
    - the professional decides which services are actually needed and provides them
    - the professional is trusted not to exploit his or her authority for unreasonable profit or gain.

- **Professional courtesy** – this is a bare minimum requirement of all business communication.

- **Expertise** – professionalism implies a level of competence that justifies financial remuneration. Incompetence is bad PR.

- **Marketing and promoting services** – accountants should not make exaggerated or defamatory claims in their marketing. This is covered in more detail in Chapter 5.

Test your understanding 2

When it comes to ethical principles, discussions often reveal that many employees think it is:

- acceptable to borrow money from the petty cash system if they have access (or their friends have access) and they are short of cash

- fine to browse the Internet or use the work telephone for unlimited numbers of personal calls

- quite appropriate to take a 'sickie' if they need a day off

- fun to invent a good story for being late or going early, and

- use work materials and tools for personal use.

Which of the fundamental principles is being flouted in these examples?

3 Threats and safeguards

3.1 Threats

Threats to compliance with the fundamental principles can be general in nature or relate to the specific circumstances of an appointment.

General categories of threats to the principles include the following:

- **The self-interest threat** – a threat to a member's integrity or objectivity may stem from a financial or other self-interest conflict.

  This could arise, for example, from a direct or indirect interest in a client or from fear of losing an engagement or having his or her employment terminated or as a consequence of undue commercial pressure from within or outside the firm.

- **The self-review threat** – there will be a threat to objectivity if any product or judgement of the member or the firm needs to be challenged or re-evaluated by him or her subsequently.

- **The advocacy threat** – there is a threat to a member's objectivity if he or she becomes an advocate for or against the position taken by the client or employer in any adversarial proceedings or situation. The degree to which this presents a threat to objectivity will depend on the individual circumstances. The presentation of only one side of the case may be compatible with objectivity provided that it is accurate and truthful.

- **The familiarity or trust threat** – is a threat that the member may become influenced by his or her
    - knowledge of the issue
    - relationship with the client or employer
    - judgement of the qualities of the client or employer to the extent that he or she becomes too trusting.

- **The intimidation threat** – the possibility that the member may become intimidated by threat, by a dominating personality, or by other pressures, actual or feared, applied by the client or employer or by another.

Each of the categories of threat may arise in relation to the member's own person or in relation to a connected person e.g. a family member or partner or person who is close for some other reason, for instance by reason of a past or present association, obligation or indebtedness.

Where members decide to accept or continue an engagement in a situation where any significant threat to objectivity has been identified, they should be able to demonstrate that they have considered the availability and effectiveness of safeguards and have reasonably concluded that those safeguards will adequately preserve their objectivity.

 Test your understanding 3

Consider each of the following threats to independence and label them according the classification given above.

- Accountancy firm does both management accounting services and auditing for the same client.

- Having audited the client firm for many years, the audit partner has become close friends with the Directors.

- Auditor owns shares in the client company.

- Directors threaten to change auditors if they do not get an unqualified audit report.

- Auditor promotes an audit client's position or opinion in an article.

3.2 Safeguards

> **🔍 Definition**
>
> Safeguards may eliminate or reduce such threats to an acceptable level. They fall into two broad categories:
>
> (i) safeguards created by the profession, legislation or regulation and
>
> (ii) safeguards in the work environment.

Safeguards created by the profession, legislation or regulation include, but are not restricted to:

(i) educational, training and experience requirements for entry into the profession

(ii) continuing professional development requirements

(iii) corporate governance regulations

(iv) professional standards

(v) professional or regulatory monitoring and disciplinary procedures

(vi) external review of the reports, returns, communications or information produced by a member and carried out by a legally empowered third party.

Safeguards in the work environment include, but are not restricted to:

(i) the employing organisation's systems of corporate oversight or other oversight structures

(ii) the employing organisation's ethics and conduct programmes

(iii) recruitment procedures in the employing organisation emphasising the importance of employing high calibre competent staff

(iv) strong internal controls

(v) appropriate disciplinary processes

(vi) leadership that stresses the importance of ethical behaviour and the expectation that employees will act in an ethical manner

(vii) policies and procedures to implement and monitor the quality of employee performance

(viii) timely communication of the employing organisation's policies and procedures, including any changes to them, to all employees and appropriate training and education on such policies and procedures

(ix)   policies and procedures to empower and encourage employees to communicate to senior levels within the employing organisation any ethical issues that concern them without fear of retribution

(x)   consultation with another appropriate professional.

The nature of the safeguards to be applied will vary depending on the circumstances. In exercising professional judgement, a member should consider what a reasonable and informed third party, having knowledge of all relevant information, including the significance of the threat and the safeguards applied, would conclude to be unacceptable.

 Test your understanding 4

From time to time, you may receive or give gifts that are meant to show friendship, appreciation or thanks from or to people who do business with your company. You know you should never accept or offer gifts or entertainment when doing so may improperly influence or appear to influence your or the recipient's business decisions. If you are involved in any stage of a decision to do business with another company or person, you also know that you must refrain from accepting or giving any gift or entertainment that may influence or appear to influence the decision to do business.

Jot down some work based safeguards that colleagues would find helpful in deciding whether to accept or reject a gift.

---

4   Dealing with ethical conflicts

Given the above principles, threats and safeguards, a process of resolving ethical conflicts can be given as follows:

Step 1: Gather information

Rumour and hearsay are insufficient evidence upon which to base a decision. The accountant should seek to gather further information to clarify the situation.

Step 2: Analysis

In analysing the scenario, the accountant should first consider the legal perspective – have any laws been broken?

Next they can look at each of the fundamental principles to see which apply and whether there is an ethical issue to resolve.

Step 3: Action

If it is clear that there is a problem to resolve, the accountant should weigh up the different courses of action:

- Is behaviour dictated by law?

- Who are the affected parties?

- Internal escalation – is there someone within the organisation who could/should be approached to discuss the matter further – for example, the Board of Directors or Audit Committee?

- If the matter is still unresolved, then they should seek professional advice without breaching confidentiality.

- External escalation – should you report the matter externally?

- Ultimately the accountant should consider resigning from the assignment.

 Test your understanding 5

You are an accountant of a large multinational organisation and have gained information about a takeover bid to acquire a rival firm.

By coincidence, a family friend is considering selling shares in this rival organisation and has asked you, as an expert in the industry, for advice on this matter.

What would you do? Which principles are affected and how?

 Test your understanding 6

You are the newly appointed accountant of a struggling manufacturing company. You have just discovered that tax benefits were wrongly claimed in previous years, reducing the tax bill and boosting profit.

You have told the Finance Director about the error but he is unwilling to disclose the misleading tax bill as by telling the tax authorities (as required by law) the organisation may go bust and 300 employees could lose their jobs.

What would you do? Which principles are affected and how?

Test your understanding 7

You are a trainee accountant in your second year of training within a small practice. A more senior trainee has been on sick leave, and you are due to go on study leave.

You have been told by your manager that, before you go on leave, you must complete a complicated task that the senior trainee was supposed to have done. The deadline suggested appears unrealistic, given the complexity of the work.

You feel that you are not sufficiently experienced to complete the work alone but your manager appears unable to offer the necessary support. You feel slightly intimidated by your manager, and also feel under pressure to be a 'team player' and help out.

However, if you try to complete the work to the required quality but fail, you could face repercussions on your return from study leave.

Required:

Analyse the scenario with particular reference to the following:

(a)   Which fundamental principles are involved?

(b)   Recommended action.

5   Summary

This chapter has introduced the concept of ethics in the business environment and has outlined the fundamental ethical principles that should be adhered to.

Also covered have been the independence threats and safeguards.

All three, the fundamental Principles, the independence threats and the safeguards to help prevent unethical behaviour are highly examinable and underpin the whole syllabus.

It is critical that you know and can apply the different principles.

6 Test your understanding answers

 Test your understanding 1

Report your client to the authorities

Examples of the points that should be considered in determining the extent to which confidential information may be disclosed are:

When the law specifically requires disclosure, it could lead to a member producing documents or giving evidence in the course of legal proceedings and disclosing to the appropriate public authorities infringements of the law.

 Test your understanding 2

In all of these examples, the employees are not being honest or straightforward – they are therefore operating against the principle of **Integrity**.

Test your understanding 3

- Self-review
- Familiarity
- Self interest
- Intimidation
- Advocacy

Test your understanding 4

Possible safeguards when considering whether to accept a gift:

- Set up clear policies and guidance for staff stating the following:

    - Cash gifts should never be accepted.

    - Do not accept a gift if it could cause you to feel an obligation.

    - Do not accept a gift from a vendor if it may give the vendor, other suppliers or subcontractors the impression that they have to provide similar gifts or favours in order to obtain company business.

    - Do not justify accepting a gift by arguing, 'Everybody else does it,' 'I deserve a break today,' or 'No one will ever find out.'

- Establish a code of ethics in the workplace that bans gifts.

- Ensure senior management are not seen accepting gifts.

 Test your understanding 5

The basic issue here is that you know that it is a bad time to sell, as the price will most likely rise when the bid is announced. However, should you tell a family friend?

(a) **Integrity** – This situation has a clear impact on your integrity – fair dealing and truthfulness.

(b) **Objectivity** – Your objectivity would be at risk if you allow a personal relationship to influence the ethical and legal responsibilities you have to your employer.

(c) **Confidentiality** – You have an obligation to refrain from disclosure of information outside the firm or employing organisation.

(d) **Professional behaviour** – You cannot compromise your professional judgement as a result of a personal relationship.

In this case, the main issue is confidentiality. In advising your family friend, you would not only risk losing your job, but are also compromising your professional judgement, integrity and future career.

You should decline to discuss the issue.

Test your understanding 6

The basic issue here is whether to cover up the tax problem to save the jobs of 300 employees.

(a) **Integrity** – By not declaring the unlawful tax benefits your integrity is clearly compromised.

(b) **Objectivity** – Firstly, you need to ascertain the facts. Your objectivity is threatened by the perceived threat of job losses. The short-term and unlawful actions to increase profit will not help the business model in the long-term.

(c) **Professional competence and due care** – By not declaring you are undermining both your professional competence as well as not acting with due care and diligence as a professional accountant.

(d) **Confidentiality** – In this case there is a legal and professional right and duty to disclose. The issue will not go away and you will be seen as complicit.

(e) **Professional behaviour** – There is a need to comply with the relevant law and regulations on this matter. By failing to declare your actions both discredits the profession and put you in disrepute.

Firstly you must be clear that there is an issue and find out the facts. Should you find that tax benefits have been unlawfully declared you should take action.

In this situation, you have to think about the long-term effects of your actions.

By not declaring the misleading tax bill the organisation might keep afloat for the moment – but it will not make the issue go away, and it will not necessarily save the jobs at risk in the long run. Doing this would severely damage your integrity and professional competence, and risk your reputation and future career.

You are legally required to disclose all information. This is clearly a tough decision to make, as jobs are at risk, but by refraining from reporting you will only worsen the situation. In addition by self-declaring there may be ways to negotiate a reduced tax bill with the authorities.

The issue needs to be discussed further with the Finance Director and then with the Board of Directors.

Test your understanding 7

(a) **Key fundamental principles affected**

    (i)   **Integrity**: Can you be open and honest about the situation?

    (ii)   **Professional competence and due care**: Would it be right to attempt to complete work that is technically beyond your abilities, without proper supervision? Is it possible to complete the work within the time available and still act diligently to achieve the required quality of output?

    (iii)   **Professional behaviour**: Can you refuse to perform the work without damaging your reputation within the practice? Alternatively, could the reputation of the practice suffer if you attempt the work?

    (iv)   **Objectivity**: Pressure from your manager, combined with the fear of repercussions, gives rise to an intimidation threat to objectivity.

(b) **Possible course of action**

You should explain to your manager that you do not have sufficient time and experience to complete the work to a satisfactory standard.

However, you should demonstrate a constructive attitude, and suggest how the problem may be resolved. (Your professional body is available to advise you in this respect.) For example, you might suggest the use of a subcontract bookkeeper.

Explore the possibility of assigning another member of staff to supervise your work.

If you feel that your manager is unsympathetic or fails to understand the issue, you should consider how best to raise the matter with the person within the practice responsible for training. It would be diplomatic to suggest to your manager that you raise the matter together, and present your respective views.

It would be unethical to attempt to complete the work if you doubt your competence.

However, simply refusing to, or resigning from your employment, would cause significant problems for both you and the practice. You could consult your professional body. If you seek advice from outside the practice (for example legal advice), then you should be mindful of the need for confidentiality as appropriate.

You should document, in detail, the steps that you take in resolving your dilemma, in case your ethical judgement is challenged in the future.

7 Additional Test your understanding questions

 Test your understanding 8

James, a member in practice, has been asked to assist a client with interviewing potential new recruits for the finance department. James has since discovered that a close personal friend of his has applied for the role.

Which fundamental principle needs to be safeguarded?

 Test your understanding 9

Explain why each of the following actions appears to be in conflict with fundamental ethical principles.

1. An advertisement for a firm of accountants states that their audit services are cheaper and more comprehensive than a rival firm.

2. An accountant prepares a set of accounts prior to undertaking the audit of those accounts.

3. A director discusses an impending share issue with colleagues at a golf club dinner.

4. The finance director asks a trainee accountant to complete the company's taxation computation following the acquisition of some foreign subsidiaries.

5. A financial accountant confirms that a report on his company is correct, even though the report omits to mention some important liabilities.

6. You believe your colleague has asked you to include what you believe to be misleading information in your forecast.

7. Your analysis of a strategic proposal suggests that profitability will be improved by making 30 people redundant.

8. You can outsource your manufacturing to a country where labour costs are much lower.

9. Your company is allowed, legally, to dump its waste into a river. This will kill all aquatic life along a 50 mile stretch.

Test your understanding 10

Explain your response to the following ethical threats.

1   Your employer tells you that you will receive a large bonus for working overtime on a project to hide liabilities from the financial statements.

2   In selecting employees for a new division, you are advised to unfairly discriminate against one section of the workforce.

3   You have been asked to prepare the management accounts for a subsidiary located in South America in accordance with specific requirements of that jurisdiction. In response to your comment that you do not understand the accounting requirements of that jurisdiction, your supervisor states "no problem, no one will notice a few thousand dollars error anyway".

 Test your understanding 11

The IT Director of ABC Ltd has asked a junior accountant within the company to undertake a cost benefit analysis of a proposed new IT system. The IT Director will use this analysis to try and convince the Board of Directors of ABC that they should invest in the new system.

As part of his analysis, the junior accountant has discovered that the new system will not run properly on ABC's existing computers. This means that ABC would have to replace the majority of their desktop computers and servers, leading to an excess of costs over benefits.

The IT Director has suggested that the junior accountant downplay the costs of replacing the IT infrastructure as he was sure that he "could find a workaround" that would allow the existing computers to use the new software, though he was currently uncertain how this would be done.

The IT Director has told the junior accountant that he 'expects' the cost benefit analysis to show a favourable result for the new system and has indicated that the junior accountant's future promotion prospects may depend on this being the case.

Required:

Explain the fundamental ethical principles that the junior accountant would be breaching if he agrees to the IT Director's request.

Test your understanding 12

Michael, a member in practice, performs account preparation services to a client called Ying Ltd. A company called Yang Ltd approaches Michael's firm and requests to become a new client. The two businesses are direct competitors and both have trade secrets which they wish to keep a secret.

Which fundamental principles are threatened?

8 Additional Test your understanding answers

 Test your understanding 8

James needs to safeguard the fundamental principle of objectivity.

His friendship may colour his judgement in favour of his friend.

 Test your understanding 9

1   Potential conflict with professional behaviour – audit services observe the same standards, therefore implying that a rival has lower standards suggests that a firm is not complying with professional standards.

2   The accountant is likely to lose objectivity because errors in the accounts made during preparation may not be identified when those accounts are reviewed.

3   As the information is likely to be confidential, discussing it in a public place is inappropriate.

4   The accountant needs to ensure that knowledge of the foreign country's taxation regime is understood prior to completing the return, otherwise there is the possibility that the appropriate professional skill will not be available.

5   There is an issue of integrity. The accountant should not allow the report to be released because it is known that the report is incorrect.

6   This is an issue of integrity. Accountants must not be associated with any form of communication or report that they know to be either materially false or misleading.

7   The reduction of the number of staff in an organisation in order to increase profit is not necessarily unethical. For example, if the business has an unnecessarily high number of employees, reducing this number may be appropriate. However, the accountant would need to ensure that the analysis was accurate, as it will impact on individual's livelihoods. If there is any uncertainty in the results, they may need to consider whether it should be disclosed. In addition, the accountant will need to be aware of the implications and should ensure that the decision makers are made aware of the potential ethical considerations.

8   Again, this is an operational decision. There are ethical concerns over the loss of current staff which the accountant should make the decision maker aware of along with the potential adverse impact on the reputation of the company.

9   Ethics involves avoiding negative impacts on the environment that the company operates in. Even though legal, the decision to dump pollution into a river is unethical due to the impact on marine life. Should an accountant be complicit in such an action, it is likely to bring the profession into disrepute.

 Test your understanding 10

Threat 1

- Do not offer the inducement!

- If necessary, follow the conflict resolution process of the employer.

- Consider the impact of the financial statements being misrepresented.

Threat 2

- Obtaining advice from the employer, professional organisation or professional advisor.

- Legal advice.

Threat 3

- Obtaining additional advice/training.

- Negotiating more time for duties.

- Obtaining assistance from someone with relevant expertise.

Test your understanding 11

If the junior accountant agrees to the IT Director's demands, he will be in breach of several of the IFAC ethical principles:

Integrity

This requires members not to be associated with any form of communication or report where the information is materially false, provided recklessly or incomplete.

The junior accountant has identified a potential problem with the proposed new system that would involve a large outflow of cash to upgrade ABC's infrastructure.

Following the IT Director's suggestion would involve the junior accountant ignoring the issue without a firm idea of how it will be resolved (the IT Director is simply suggesting a vague 'workaround').

This means that the report will be incomplete and misleading to its users.

Objectivity

This requires accountants to ensure that their judgement is not compromised because of bias or conflict of interest.

The junior accountant is only likely to agree to the IT Director's demands because failing to do so could jeopardise his career. This would clearly be acting in his own self-interest.

Professional competence and due care

This requires accountants to follow all applicable technical and professional standards when providing services.

The junior accountant is aware that the cost benefit analysis, when undertaken properly, shows an unfavourable result for the new IT system.

Failing to use the correctly obtained result could be seen as a failure to meet professional and technical standards.

Professional behaviour

This principle requires accountants to avoid any activities that might bring the profession into disrepute.

If the junior accountant is found to have knowingly misled the Board of Directors into buying a system that is not cost effective, it would clearly damage confidence in the accountancy profession as a whole.

Test your understanding 12

Objectivity and confidentiality.

Professional considerations

2

Introduction

Being a member of the AAT is more than a qualification. The AAT is well recognised and respected throughout a wide range of businesses and, in order to maintain this reputation and to continue to offer quality training and support, the AAT require their members to have a professional and ethical approach throughout their lives.

The view of the accounting profession is that the ongoing development of knowledge, judgement and expertise is essential in today's business environment. All members owe it to themselves, and their fellow members, to ensure that they are professionally up-to-date so that the reputation of their qualification is safeguarded.

It is particularly important that professional accountants act in this way, especially given the fact that anyone can set themselves up as offering accountancy services, even if they are not qualified.

ASSESSMENT CRITERIA	
1.1	Explain why it is important to act ethically
1.2	Explain how to act ethically
1.3	Explain the importance of values, culture and codes of practice/conduct
2.1	Explain the ethical code's conceptual framework of principles, threats, safeguards and professional judgement
2.2	Explain the importance of acting with integrity
2.4	Explain the importance of behaving professionally
2.5	Explain the importance of being competent and acting with due care
3.1	Distinguish between ethical and unethical behaviour
3.2	Analyse a situation using the conceptual framework and the conflict resolution process
3.3	Develop an ethical course of action

CONTENTS	
1	The role of a professional accountant
2	The objectives of the profession
3	The role of professional bodies
4	AAT's sponsors and other industry-related bodies
5	Keeping up to date
6	AAT disciplinary process

1 The role of a professional accountant

Members serve in many different capacities and should demonstrate their objectivity in varying circumstances. Members in practice undertake professional services. Other members as employees prepare financial statements, perform internal audit services and serve in financial management capacities in the accountancy profession, industry, commerce, public sector and education. Members also educate and train those who aspire to admission to the AAT.

1.1 Responsibility to the public

A professional accountant's responsibility is not exclusively to satisfy the needs of an individual client or employer. A distinguishing mark of a profession is acceptance of its responsibility to the public.

 Definition

The **public interest** is defined as the collective wellbeing of the community of people and institutions the professional accountant serves.

The accountancy profession's public consists of employers, creditors, clients, governments, employees, investors, the business and financial community and others who rely on its objectivity and integrity to maintain the orderly functioning of commerce. For example:

- financial managers serve in various financial management capacities in organisations and contribute to the efficient and effective use of the organisation's resources

- internal auditors provide assurance about a sound internal control system which enhances the reliability of the external financial information of the employer

- independent auditors help to maintain the integrity and efficiency of the financial statements presented to financial institutions in partial support for loans and to shareholders for obtaining capital

- tax experts help to establish confidence and efficiency in the tax system

- management consultants have a responsibility toward the public interest in advocating sound management decision-making.

This reliance imposes a public interest responsibility on the accountancy profession.

Professional accountants can remain in this advantageous position only by continuing to provide these services at a level that demonstrates that public confidence is firmly founded. It is in the best interest of the accountancy profession to make known to users that the services it provides are executed at the highest level of performance and in accordance with ethical requirements set to ensure such performance.

1.2   Statutory regulated functions

Professional accountants in public practice should be free of any interest which might be regarded, whatever its actual effect, as being incompatible with integrity, objectivity and independence.

Members of the AAT who provide accounting, taxation or related consultancy services on a self-employed basis in the UK must register on the scheme for self-employed members and comply with the Guidelines and Regulations for Self-employed members.

Statutory regulated ('reserved') functions

In accordance with the AAT's Code of Professional Ethics, unless appropriately authorised by a regulatory body established under statutory authority, members may not perform the following functions in the UK:

- external audit of UK limited companies and any other prescribed organisation with the provisions of the Companies Acts

- external audit of other bodies that require the services of a registered auditor

- activities regulated by the Financial Conduct Authority (FCA) including the undertaking of investment business and the provision of corporate finance advice to clients

- insolvency practice in accordance with the provisions of the relevant insolvency legislation.

The following three sections detail the work which an AAT member is open to practice, such as: final account preparation, internal audit, management accounts and tax advice.

Note that membership of a professional accountancy body is not required for a person to offer services as an accountant in the UK.

1.3 Preparing financial statements

In compliance with applicable laws, and in accordance with accepted accounting standards, accountants have an obligation to make full, fair, accurate, timely and understandable disclosure when preparing financial records and statements, and when submitting or filing reports and documents to the regulatory authorities.

When members are performing their duties, they must act in good faith, responsibly, with due care, competence and diligence, without misrepresenting material facts or allowing their independent judgement to be subordinated.

They must do this in order to ensure that to the best of their knowledge the books, records, accounts and financial statements are maintained accurately and in reasonable detail. These should appropriately reflect the organisation's transactions, be honestly and accurately reflected in its publicly available reports and communications and conform to applicable legal requirements and systems of internal controls, including the organisation's disclosure policy.

1.4 Internal audit

 Definition

Internal auditing is an independent, objective assurance and consulting activity designed to add value and improve an organisation's operations.

As we have already noted, internal auditors provide assurance about a sound internal control system, which enhances the reliability of the external financial information of the employer.

Whatever the nature of the professional services they provide, members may be exposed to situations that involve the possibility of pressures and threats being exerted on them. These pressures and threats may impair their objectivity, and hence their independence.

Objectivity is essential to the audit function. Therefore, accountants performing internal audit services should not develop and install procedures, prepare records, or engage in any other activity which they would normally review or assess and which could reasonably be construed to compromise their independence.

1.5 Financial management services

Financial management and consulting services are advisory in nature, and are generally performed at the specific request of an engagement client.

When performing consulting services the accountant should maintain objectivity and not assume management responsibility.

 Test your understanding 1

State TWO of the three statutory regulated or reserved areas of accountancy and finance.

2 The objectives of the profession

2.1 AAT Guidelines

The accountancy profession, including the part represented by the AAT, is committed to the following objectives:

- The mastering of particular skills and techniques acquired through learning and education and maintained through continuing professional development.

- Development of an ethical approach to work as well as to employers and clients. This is acquired by experience and professional supervision under training and is safeguarded by strict ethical and disciplinary guidelines.

- Acknowledgement of duties to society as a whole in addition to duties to the employer or the client.

- An outlook which is essentially objective, obtained by being fair minded and free from conflicts of interest.

- Rendering services to the highest standards of conduct and performance.

- Achieving acceptance by the public that members provide accountancy services in accordance with these high standards and requirements.

These six objectives can be found in the AAT's code of professional ethics and underpin the code.

3 The role of professional bodies

(Note: The role of professional bodies is not explicitly mentioned in the new syllabus. It is included as background information for the professional accountant. It is linked in this respect to the wider business context and to assessment objective 1, 2 and 4.)

There are a number of professional bodies, both international and national, that are relevant to the professional accountant's work.

3.1 The International Federation of Accountants (IFAC)

The role of the IFAC is to protect the public interest by developing high quality international standards, promoting strong ethical values and encouraging quality practice.

3.2 IFAC's International Ethics Standards Board for Accountants (IESBA)

IFAC's International Ethics Standards Board for Accountants (IESBA) is an independent standard-setting board that develops and issues, in the public interest, high-quality ethical standards and other pronouncements for professional accountants worldwide.

The board also provides adoption and implementation support, promotes good ethical practices globally, and fosters international debate on ethical issues faced by accountants.

3.3 The International Audit and Assurance Standards Board (IAASB)

The IAASB is a division of IFAC and is responsible for developing, setting and promoting International Standards on Auditing (ISAs).

3.4 The International Accounting Standards Board (IASB)

The IASB is an independent body responsible for developing, setting and promoting International Financial Reporting Standards.

3.5 The Financial Reporting Council (FRC)

The Financial Reporting Council (FRC) is the UK's independent regulator responsible for promoting high quality corporate governance and reporting to foster investment.

The main areas where most accountants experience the work of the FRC are in terms of accounting and auditing standards:

- The Board of the FRC issues UK versions of International Standards on Auditing where appropriate, taking advice from the Audit & Assurance Council (part of the FRC)

- The Board of the FRC also issues UK versions of International Financial Reporting Standards where appropriate, taking advice from the Accounting Council (part of the FRC).

Note: The Accounting Council replaced the Accounting Standards Board.

3.6 The Conduct Committee

The Conduct Committee is part of the FRC and provides independent oversight of professional disciplinary issues, together with oversight of the regulation of accountants and actuaries in the UK and Republic of Ireland.

Note: The Conduct Committee replaced the Professional Oversight Board.

 Test your understanding 2

Describe the difference between the Accounting Council and the Audit and Assurance Council.

 Test your understanding 3

Which body sets global ethical standards for accountants?

 4 **AAT's sponsors and other industry-related bodies**

4.1 Sponsoring bodies

The AAT is sponsored by the following accountancy bodies:

- **CIPFA** – The Chartered Institute of Public Finance and Accountancy
- **ICAEW** – The Institute for Chartered Accountants in England and Wales
- **CIMA** – The Chartered Institute of Management Accountants
- **ICAS** – The Institute for Chartered Accountants in Scotland

4.2 The Consultative Committee of Accountancy Bodies

The Consultative Committee of Accountancy Bodies (CCAB) provides a forum in which matter affecting the profession can be discussed, and enables the profession to speak with a unified voice in the UK and ROI.

The CCAB is a collective committee and includes:

- **ICAEW**
- **ICAS**
- **CAI** – Chartered Accountants Ireland
- **ACCA** – The Association of Chartered Certified Accountants
- **CIPFA**

4.3 Her Majesty's Revenue and Customs (HMRC)

- HM Revenue & Customs (HMRC) was formed in 2005, following the merger of the Inland Revenue and HM Customs and Excise.
- They ensure the correct tax is paid at the right time.
- They collect and administer direct (e.g. Income Tax) and indirect tax (e.g. VAT), and pay child benefit and tax credits.

4.4 The Financial Conduct Authority (FCA)

The FCA regulates the financial services industry in the UK.

The aim of the FCA is to

- protect consumers,
- ensure the financial services industry remains stable and
- promote healthy competition between financial services providers.

It has been given a wide range of rule-making, investigatory and enforcement powers.

4.5   The Prudential Regulatory Authority (PRA)

Part of the Bank of England, the Prudential Regulation Authority (PRA) is responsible for the prudential regulation and supervision of banks, building societies, credit unions, insurers and major investment firms.

Note: The FCA and PRA have taken over some of the roles previously undertaken by the Financial Services Authority (FSA).

4.6   National Crime Agency (NCA)

The National Crime Agency (NCA) is a national police unit that has a wide remit and tackles serious organised crime that affects the UK and its citizens.

This includes:

- Serious and organised crime
- Border policing
- Child exploitation and online protection (CEOP)
- Major gun crime
- Fraud
- Cyber crime
- Money laundering.

 Test your understanding 4

Which of the following professional bodies is **not** a sponsor of the AAT?

A   ACCA

B   ICAS

C   ICAEW

D   CIPFA

 Test your understanding 5

Describe **TWO** aims of the Financial Conduct Authority (FCA).

5 Keeping up to date

5.1 Why is keeping up to date important?

Having up-to-date technical knowledge means the professional accountant can act with technical and professional competence in providing services to clients and service to an employer.

Failure to keep up to date is thus a breach of ethical principle of professional competence, which states:

> A member has a continuing duty to maintain professional knowledge and skill at the level required to ensure that a client or employer receives competent professional service based on current developments in practice, legislation and techniques.

Areas in which up-to-date technical knowledge for an accountant is critical include the following:

- Changes in reporting and auditing standards
- Changes in ethical codes
- Changes in tax and companies legislation
- Changes in relevant criminal law including bribery, fraud, money laundering
- Changes in regulation of accounting, reporting, tax compliance, audit, the accountancy and finance profession.

5.2 How to keep up to date

An accountant can keep up to date by a mixture of the following:

- Reading professional journals
- Enrolling on update courses
- Complying with continuing professional development (CPD) requirements for qualified professional accountants.

It is recognised that the best and most efficient way for members to keep up to date, maintain and improve their skills is through a planned programme of activities.

This implies that individuals accept responsibility for their own development by drawing on a combination of self-education and using well-established and credible providers of training and education.

5.3 Continuing Professional Development (CPD)

 Definition

Continuing Professional Development (CPD) can be defined as 'the continuous maintenance, development and enhancement of the professional and personal knowledge, skills and ability, often termed competence, which members of certain professions require throughout their working lives'.

- **Continuing** because learning never ceases, regardless of age or seniority.

- **Professional** because it is focused on personal competence in a professional role.

- **Development** because its goal is to improve personal performance and enhance career progression and is much wider than just formal training courses.

There are two strands to CPD:

(i) update CPD, which ensures professional competence and prevents technical obsolescence within the member's field of work

(ii) developmental CPD, which provides new knowledge, broadens skills and opens up new career opportunities.

In any one year, you could be undertaking one or both strands. The term 'professional' is deemed to include both personal and technical competences.

5.4 The CPD cycle

The CPD cycle has four stages:

1 **Assess – identify the skills and knowledge that you already have**

This requires a critical analysis of work experience (skills practised and demonstrated) and previous education and study (knowledge).

2 **Plan – consider where you are heading in your career, identify the 'gap' and plan how to achieve your objectives**

Determine what your career goals and aspirations are, and consider the job roles within your industry or profession and the skills, knowledge and attributes they require.

By completing the previous steps you will have identified the areas in which you need further skill development or knowledge to achieve your career goal or aspiration. The 'gap' is your development or training need.

3   **Action – undertake CPD activities**

The action stage is the implementation of the plan – for example, attending update courses, reading journals, etc.

4   **Evaluate**

When reflecting on your activities you should consider whether or not you have experienced personal or business benefits from your efforts through the practical application of what you have learnt.

Licensed members (i.e. running your own practice) need to complete CPD twice a year (https://www.aat.org.uk/about-aat/applying-for-an-aat-licence/licence-conditions) but normal CPD is at least once every 12 months.

5.5   What counts as CPD?

CPD is any kind of learning as long as the subject and activity are relevant to your professional role and learning needs, and there are significant learning outcomes. It is something you will almost certainly already be doing as part of your everyday working life.

A CPD scheme will probably mean a certain amount of your learning will be in the form of 'structured' CPD. Structured CPD is learning where you get guidance from another knowledgeable person (e.g. a lecturer, trainer, speaker at a conference or seminar, experienced practitioner).

It also means being able to participate by taking part in exercises, practice the skills being learnt, ask questions etc. Other activities that may qualify as structured learning include service as a member on a technical committee, writing technical articles, or presenting on a structured course (but not repeat presentations). In general, however, one single repetitive activity should not constitute the extent of a member's CPD activity.

Apart from participation in structured learning activities, there is a continuing need for members to keep abreast of a wide range of developments affecting their profession, clients and employers.

This is achieved through unstructured CPD activities, such as regularly reading professional journals and the financial and business press. Other unstructured activities may include the use of video or audiotapes, computer based learning programmes, distance learning or alternative forms of learning where there is no interaction with other individuals and no assessment is provided.

Structured CPD	Unstructured CPD
• In house training	• Reading professional/ technical articles
• Other professional bodies	• Educational videos/tapes
• University courses	• Specific reading material that relates to practical work
• Conferences both local and international	• Distance learning (with no assessment)
• Branch courses	
• National courses	
• Assessed distance learning	
• Outside providers	
• Other structured courses	

Almost everyone's job is about much more than simply applying a particular set of technical knowledge and skills. Communicating with customers and colleagues, organising time and workload, delegating work to others and maintaining records are just some vital skills for all professionals. This is why the AAT does not dictate what subjects you should cover. They recognise that CPD covers a wide range of knowledge and skills. You can decide the relevant subjects for your CPD. But, as an AAT member you are responsible for making sure you are properly up to date and competent in all the key areas of your role.

 Test your understanding 6

Glenda works in practice as a tax specialist.

Suggest THREE ways Glenda could keep her technical knowledge up to date.

 Test your understanding 7

Explain the difference between structured and unstructured CPD.

6 AAT disciplinary process

6.1 Grounds for disciplinary action

It shall be a ground for disciplinary action if a member is guilty of misconduct.

 Definition

Misconduct. Can be defined as a member having conducted him/herself in such a manner as would in the opinion of the association, prejudice his/her status as a member or reflect adversely on the reputation of the Association; or having acted in serious or repeated breach of the Articles or of any rules, regulations or bye-laws.

 Example 1 – Misconduct

The following shall be conclusive proof of misconduct:

- A member has, before a court of competent jurisdiction, pleaded guilty to or has been found guilty of an indictable offence.

- A member has, in the absence of exceptional mitigating circumstances, become bankrupt or has entered into any formal arrangement with his/her creditors.

- A member has not complied with the Money Laundering Regulations from time to time in force.

- A member has not complied with the Association's policy on continuing professional development (CPD).

- A member has unreasonably refused to cooperate with an investigation carried out in accordance with these Regulations.

- A member in practice has failed to renew his/her practicing licence before the date of expiry.

- A member has repeatedly failed to reply to correspondence from the Association.

6.2 Disciplinary action

Any one or more of the following actions may be recommended by the Investigations Team as is considered appropriate having regard to the nature and seriousness of the misconduct, the member's character and past record and to any other relevant circumstances.

In the case of a full or fellow member (but not an affiliate or student member) that he or she:

- Be expelled from the Association

- Have his/her membership of the Association suspended

- Have his/her practising Licence withdrawn

- Be declared ineligible for a practising Licence

- Have his/her fellow member status removed (if applicable)

- Be reprimanded or severely reprimanded

- Be fined, subject to a maximum level

- Give a written undertaking to refrain from continuing or repeating the misconduct in question.

In the case of an affiliate or student member (but not a full or fellow member) that he or she:

- Be declared unfit to become a full member

- Have his/her registration as a student withdrawn

- Be reprimanded or severely reprimanded

- Be fined, subject to a maximum level

- Be debarred from sitting the association's assessments for such period as shall be determined

- Have a relevant assessment result declared null and void

- Give a written undertaking to refrain from continuing or repeating the misconduct in question.

📝 Test your understanding 8

Why does the AAT have a disciplinary process?

A   To deter members from criminal activities.

B   To provide jobs for AAT head office staff.

C   To comply with government legislation.

D   To maintain public confidence in the accountancy profession.

---

7 Summary

This chapter has introduced the concept of professionalism what that means for the professional accountant.

The AAT qualification is highly regarded and the objectives of the professional qualifications are an important area of the syllabus.

The roles of different bodies will come up in the computer based project so it is vital that you learn the details here, rather than relying on common sense.

CPD is the means by which members of professional bodies maintain, improve and broaden their knowledge and skills and develop the personal qualities required in their professional lives.

Your CPD should be driven by your need to improve or maintain competence in the areas needed to perform your role. Therefore, your CPD activities should relate to the knowledge and skills that you, as an individual, require. CPD can cover not only technical core accounting capabilities, but also areas such as communication, personnel management, project and operations management, information technology, language and culture – anything that develops your ability to perform your role as a professional.

8 Test your understanding answers

 ## Test your understanding 1

Any two of the following:

- Audit
- Investment business, or
- Insolvency.

 ## Test your understanding 2

Both the Accounting Council and the Audit and Assurance Council are parts of the Financial Reporting Council (FRC) and advise the board on adapting international standards for use in the UK.

The difference is that

- the Accounting Council advises on potential amendments to International Financial Reporting Standards (IFRSs)
- the Audit and Assurance Council advises on potential amendments to International Standards on Auditing (ISAs).

 ## Test your understanding 3

The International Ethics Standards Board for Accountants (IESBA), although an alternative acceptable answer in the exam would be the International Federation of Accountants (IFAC).

 ## Test your understanding 4

A

The ACCA is not a sponsoring body of the AAT.

Test your understanding 5

The aims of the Financial Conduct Authority (FCA) are as follows (any TWO required):

- Protect consumers
- Ensure the financial services industry remains stable, and
- Promote healthy competition between financial services providers.

 Test your understanding 6

Glenda could keep her tax knowledge up to date through the following means:

- Read professional journals.
- Attend technical update courses.
- Comply with CPD requirements

 Test your understanding 7

- Structured CPD is learning where you get guidance from another knowledgeable person (e.g. a lecturer, trainer, speaker at a conference or seminar, experienced practitioner).
- Unstructured CPD is learning where there is no interaction with other individuals and no assessment is provided, such as regularly reading professional journals and the financial and business press.

 Test your understanding 8

D

To maintain public confidence in the accountancy profession.

9 Additional Test your understanding questions

 Test your understanding 9

Describe the role of the Financial Reporting Council.

 Test your understanding 10

Identify whether each of the following professional accountancy bodies are a member of The Consultative Committee of Accountancy Bodies (CCAB) by sorting them into the appropriate box.

Member of CCAB	Not a member of CCAB

ICAEW   ICAS   FRC   IFAC   CAI   ACCA   CIMA   CIPFA   AAT

 Test your understanding 11

In the UK, which part of the Financial Reporting Council has direct responsibility for advising on setting new accounting standards or amending existing ones in response to evolving business practices, new economic developments and deficiencies being identified in current practice?

Test your understanding 12

(a) Which of the following is NOT a sponsoring body of the AAT?

    A   ICAEW

    B   ICAS

    C   FRC

    D   CIMA

(b) Which of the following IS a sponsoring body of the AAT?

    A   CAI

    B   ACCA

    C   IFAC

    D   CIPFA

(c) The role of IFAC is to protect the public interest by developing high quality international standards, promoting strong ethical values and encouraging quality practice?

    A   True

    B   False

Test your understanding 13

The accountancy profession is committed to which of the following objectives?

A   Rendering services to an adequate level of service.

B   The mastering of particular skills and techniques acquired through learning and education and maintaining these through CPD.

C   Development of an ethical approach to work, but not including employers or clients.

Test your understanding 14

Which of the following is not an AAT student member disciplinary punishment:

A   Unlimited fine.

B   Expulsion from the AAT student membership.

C   Being reprimanded.

D   Being severely reprimanded.

 Test your understanding 15

Answer the following questions by selecting the correct option.

(a)   When do you have to comply with the AAT's rules/regulations

- Once you pass your final exam.

- After you receive your AAT certificate.

- As soon as you register as a student.

(b)   Which of the following is the AAT's ultimate punishment for student wrongdoing:

- Being made to retake your exams.

- Being declared unfit to become a member.

- Being fined.

- Being severely reprimanded.

10 Additional Test your understanding answers

 Test your understanding 9

The role of the Financial Reporting Council is as follows:

- Promotes good financial reporting in the UK and ROI.

- Issues UK versions of ISAs and IFRSs where appropriate.

 Test your understanding 10

Identify whether each of the following professional accountancy bodies are a member of The Consultative Committee of Accountancy Bodies (CCAB) by sorting them into the appropriate box.

Member of CCAB	Not a member of CCAB
ICAEW	AAT
ICAS	FRC
CAI	IFAC
ACCA	CIMA
CIPFA	

 Test your understanding 11

The Accounting Council.

Test your understanding 12

(a) **C** – FRC

(b) **D** – CIPFA

(c) **A** – True

 Test your understanding 13

B

The accountancy profession is committed to the mastering of particular skills and techniques acquired through learning and education and maintaining these through CPD.

 Test your understanding 14

A

An unlimited fine is not an AAT student member disciplinary punishment.

 Test your understanding 15

(a) You have to comply with the AAT's rules/regulations as soon as you register as a student.

(b) The AAT's ultimate punishment for student wrongdoing is being declared unfit to become a member.

Legal considerations – I

3

Introduction

As well as being influenced by ethical principles and professional considerations, the professional accountant must ensure compliance with relevant legislation, thus reducing firms' risk exposure.

This chapter focuses primarily on the issues of money laundering and whistleblowing.

ASSESSMENT CRITERIA

1.1 Explain why it is important to act ethically

1.2 Explain how to act ethically

1.3 Explain the importance of values, culture and codes of practice/conduct

2.1 Explain the ethical code's conceptual framework of principles, threats, safeguards and professional judgement

3.2 Analyse a situation using the conceptual framework and the conflict resolution process

3.3 Develop an ethical course of action

4.1 Analyse a given situation in light of money laundering law and regulations

4.2 Identify the relevant body to which questionable behaviour must be reported

4.3 Report suspected money laundering in accordance with the regulations

4.4 Decide when and how to report unethical behaviour by employers, colleagues or clients/customers

CONTENTS

1 Risk

2 Civil and criminal law

3 What is money laundering and terrorist financing?

4 Procedure for reporting money laundering

5 Tipping off

6 Customer Due Diligence

7 Whistleblowing

1   Risk

(Note: Risk is not explicitly mentioned as a topic in the syllabus. It is included as background information for the professional accountant. It is linked in this respect to the wider business context and to assessment objective 1, 2 and 4.)

1.1   Risk

All businesses face risk and uncertainty.

For example:

- Political risks: the risk a host government may act against you as a company – e.g. stop repatriation of funds.

- Economic risks: changing economic conditions – e.g. a recession.

- Social risks: change in tastes, demography – e.g. a clothing item is no longer considered fashionable.

- Technological risks: e.g. a product may become obsolete due to technological advances.

🔍 Definitions – Risk

There are many different definitions of risk including the following:

1   The unexpected variability or volatility of future cash flows and returns.

2   The probability or threat of quantifiable damage, injury, liability, loss, or any other negative occurrence that is caused by external or internal vulnerabilities, and that may be avoided through pre-emptive action.

3   The probability of something happening multiplied by the resulting cost or benefit if it does. Risk = probability × impact.

4   The effect of uncertainty on objectives.

Risk management is a key aspect of running a business and accountants can be involved in many aspects of this, ranging from identifying and assessing risks, to setting up safeguards and internal controls to reduce risk.

Test your understanding 1

Suggest FOUR areas of business risk exposure for a farmer.

1.2 Operational risk?

Within the Ethics for Accountants syllabus we are most interested in **operational** risks.

Definition – Operational risk

'the risk of losses resulting from inadequate or failed internal processes, people and systems, or external events'

(Basel Committee on Banking Supervision)

Operational risk refers to potential losses that might arise in business operations. Operational risks include risks of fraud or employee malfeasance, which are explained in more detail later.

Organisations have internal control systems to manage operational risks.

The following are examples of specific areas of operational risk to a business:

- **Reputational Risk** – any kind of threat to the way in which the company is perceived.

- **Litigation Risk** – possible loss or damage which is a consequence of legal action.

- **Process Risk** – possible losses resulting from poorly designed business processes.

In particular Ethics for Accountants will focus on risks due to the following:

- Money laundering and terrorist financing – covered in this chapter.

- Fraud and theft – covered in Chapter 4.

- Bribery – covered in Chapter 4.

- Other unethical behaviour – covered in Chapters 1 and 5.

- Pollution and other unsustainable practices – covered in Chapter 6.

> ### ✍ Test your understanding 2
>
> A business is concerned about adverse publicity in the national press over a recent pollution incident. What type of operational risk would this be described as?
>
> A   Regulatory risk
>
> B   Event risk
>
> C   Process risk
>
> D   Reputational risk

2   Civil and criminal law

(Note: Types of law is not explicitly mentioned as a topic in the syllabus. It is included as background information for the professional accountant. It is linked in this respect to the wider business context and to assessment objective 1, 2 and 4.)

2.1   Introduction

Law is necessary in every society, to enable the harmonious coexistence of its members. As the population expands, as people live more closely together in towns and cities, and as technology becomes more powerful, law has to become more detailed and explicit.

In all modern societies, legal rules fall into two fundamental categories:

1   **Criminal**

    Criminal law relates to conduct of which the State disapproves and which it seeks to control. It is a form of public law.

    In criminal law the case is brought by the State, in the name of the Crown. A criminal case will be reported as Regina (or R.) v X, where Regina is the Latin for 'queen' and R. is the accepted abbreviation.

    Examples include the crimes of theft, money laundering, terrorist financing, bribery and fraud, covered in this chapter and the next.

2 Civil

Civil law is a form of private law and involves the relationship between individual citizens.

In civil law the action is brought by the claimant, who is seeking a remedy. The case will be referred to by the names of the parties involved in the dispute, such as Brown v Smith. A civil action is known as a 'lawsuit', or 'suit', and the verb is 'to sue'.

Examples include breach of contract, negligence and breach of trust.

2.2 Differences between civil and criminal law

The key differences between criminal and civil law are as follows:

	Criminal	**Civil**
Purpose	The enforcement of particular forms of behaviour by the State, which acts to ensure compliance.	To settle disputes between individuals and to provide remedies.
Object	To regulate society by the threat of punishment.	Usually financial compensation to put the claimant in the position he would have been in had the wrong not occurred.
Burden of proof	Guilt must be shown beyond reasonable doubt (higher standard of proof).	Liability must be shown on the balance of probabilities (lower standard of proof).
Result	If found guilty, the criminal court will sentence the accused and it may fine him or impose a period of imprisonment. If innocent the accused will be acquitted.	The civil court will order the defendant to pay damages or it may order some other remedy, e.g. specific performance or injunction.

Example 1 – Criminal and civil law

Suppose Nagini works as an accountant for Tom and makes a mistake on a task that exceeds her professional expertise.

Suppose further that this results in Tom receiving a fine for the mistake.

Tom could seek compensation from Nagini on two grounds:

- For breach of contract.
- For professional negligence.

 Example 2 – Criminal and civil law

Suppose you are driving too fast and have a car crash.

- You might be prosecuted under criminal law for speeding and /or dangerous driving.
- The other party in the accident might try to sue you for damages under civil law.

 Test your understanding 3

What is the normal burden of proof placed upon the prosecution in a civil case?

A   Balance of probabilities

B   Beyond every conceivable doubt

C   Beyond any doubt

D   Beyond reasonable doubt

3 What is money laundering and terrorist financing?

3.1 Money laundering

 Definitions

Money laundering is the process by which criminally obtained money or other assets (criminal property) are exchanged for 'clean' money or other assets with no obvious link to their criminal origins. It also covers money, however come by, which is used to fund terrorism.

Criminal property is property which was obtained as a result of criminal conduct and the person knows or suspects that it was obtained from such conduct. It may take any form, including money or money's worth, securities, tangible property and intangible property.

In simple terms:

- Criminals make money through illegal actions.

- This money can be traced by the police so criminals try and stop it being tracked by buying and selling valuable items.

- The proceeds are constantly being re-invested in something else and it becomes very difficult to trace the money.

- 'Dirty cash' becomes a nice clean cheque.

There are three acknowledged phases to money laundering:

- **Placement**

  Cash generated from crime is placed in the financial system, for example paid into a bank account. This is the point when proceeds of crime are most apparent and at risk of detection.

- **Layering**

  Once proceeds of crime are in the financial system, layering obscures their origins by passing the money through complex transactions. These often involve different entities like companies and trusts and can take place in multiple jurisdictions.

- **Integration**

  Once the origin of the funds has been obscured, the criminal is able to make the funds reappear as legitimate funds or assets. They will invest funds in legitimate businesses or other forms of investment such as property.

Activities related to money laundering include:

- Acquiring, using or possessing criminal property.

- Handling the proceeds of crimes such as theft, fraud and tax evasion.

- Being knowingly involved in any way with criminal or terrorist property.

- Entering into arrangements to facilitate laundering criminal or terrorist property.

- Investing the proceeds of crimes in other financial products.

- Investing the proceeds of crimes through the acquisition of property/assets.

- Transferring criminal property.

3.2   Terrorist financing

🔍 Definitions

Terrorism is the use or threat of action designed to influence government, or to intimidate any section of the public, or to advance a political, religious or ideological cause where the action would involve violence, threats to health and safety, damage to property or disruption of electronic systems.

Terrorist financing is fund raising, possessing or dealing with property or facilitating someone else to do so, when intending, knowing or suspecting or having reasonable cause to suspect that it is intended for the purposes of terrorism.

Terrorist property is money or property likely to be used for terrorist purposes or the proceeds of commissioning or carrying out terrorist acts.

The definition of 'terrorist property' means that all dealings with funds or property which are likely to be used for the purposes of terrorism, even if the funds are 'clean' in origin, is a terrorist financing offence.

Money laundering involves the proceeds of crime while terrorist financing may involve both legitimate property and the proceeds of crime.

3.3 UK anti-money laundering legislation (AMLL)

The AMLL consist of:

- The Proceeds of Crime Act 2002 as amended (POCA)

- The Money Laundering Regulations 2007 (MLR)

- The Terrorism Act 2000 as amended (TA)

The UK legislation on money laundering and terrorist financing applies to the proceeds of conduct that are a criminal offence in the UK and most conduct occurring elsewhere that would have been an offence if it had taken place in the UK.

3.4 To whom does the AMLL apply?

Anyone can commit a money laundering offence.

However, the Proceeds Of Crime Act (POCA) and the Terrorism Act (TA) include additional offences which can be committed by **individuals working in the regulated sector,** that is by people providing specified professional services such as accountancy.

This means that an **accountant** (i.e. an AAT member in practice) will be personally liable for breaching POCA and/or TA if he or she acts as an accountancy service provider while turning a 'blind eye' to a client's suspect dealings.

The Money Laundering Regulation (MLR) imposes duties on 'relevant persons' (sole traders and firms (not employees) operating within the regulated sector) to establish and maintain practice, policies and procedures to detect and deter activities relating to money laundering and terrorist financing. It is the sole trader or firm which will be liable therefore for any breach of the MLR.

The practice, policies and procedures required by the MLR of accountancy service providers include:

- Customer Due Diligence on clients

- reporting money laundering/terrorist financing

- record keeping.

Materiality or **de minimis** exceptions are not available in relation to either money laundering or terrorist financing offences – meaning no amount is too small not to bother about.

Definition

'de minimis' means **'considered trivial'**.

In this context it means that all potential offences must be reported as no amount is too small to be of consequence.

3.5 What are the specific money laundering and terrorist financing offences?

Under the POCA, the three money laundering offences are

- s327 – Concealing, disguising, converting, transferring or removing criminal property.

- s328 – Taking part in an arrangement to facilitate the acquisition, use or control of criminal property.

- s329 – Acquiring, using or possessing criminal property.

 Definition

The **statutory** definition of **money laundering** is 'an act which constitutes an offence under sections 327, 328 or 329 of POCA'.

Conviction of any of these offences is punishable by up to 14 years imprisonment and/or an unlimited fine.

4 Procedure for reporting money laundering

4.1 Summary of key points

- **Suspicious activity reports (SARs)** submitted by the regulated sector are an important source of information used by **NCA** in meeting its harm reduction agenda, and by law enforcement more generally.

- Businesses are required to have procedures which provide for the nomination of a person, this person is called a **Money Laundering Reporting Officer (MRLO)** to receive disclosures (internal reports) and requires that everyone in the business complies with the Proceeds of Crime Act (POCA) in terms of reporting knowledge, suspicion or reasonable grounds for knowledge or suspicion of money laundering.

- Without the presence within an organisation of an MLRO an individual MUST report directly to the National Crime Agency (NCA). **Note:** The NCA was previously known as the Serious Organised Crime Agency (SOCA).

- An individual other than the MLRO fulfils his reporting obligations by making an internal report to his MLRO.

- The MLRO is responsible for assessing internal reports, making further inquiries if need be (either within the business or using public domain information), and, if appropriate, filing SARs with NCA.

- When reports are properly made they are 'protected' under POCA in that nothing in them shall be taken to breach confidentiality.

- A person who considers he may have engaged or is about to engage in money laundering, should make an 'authorised' disclosure. Such a disclosure, provided it is made before the act is carried out, or is made as soon as possible on the initiative of that person after the act is done and with good reason being shown for the delay, may provide a defence against charges of money laundering. When properly made such reports shall not be taken to breach confidentiality.

4.2 An accountant's duty to report

POCA and TA impose an obligation on accountants (individuals within the regulated sector, including those involved in providing accountancy services to clients i.e. AAT members in practice), to submit in defined circumstances:

- An internal report to a Money Laundering Reporting Officer (MLRO), by those employed in a group practice.

- A Suspicious Activity Report (SAR) to the National Crime Agency (NCA), by sole practitioners and MLROs.

There are two circumstances when a required disclosure in an internal report or a SAR, collectively referred to below as a report, must be made by an accountant:

1 When the accountant wishes to provide services in relation to property which it is actually known or suspected relates to money laundering or terrorist financing. In such circumstances, the reporter must indicate in the report that consent is required to provide such services, and must refrain from doing so until consent is received.

2   When the accountant actually knows or suspects, or there are reasonable (objective) grounds for knowing or suspecting, that another person is engaged in money laundering or terrorist financing, whether or not he or she wishes to act for such person. The person in question could be a client, a colleague or a third party.

4.3   Required disclosure

The required disclosure which must be included in a suspicious activity report (SAR) is as follows:

- The identity of the suspect (if known).

- The information or other matter on which the knowledge or suspicion of money laundering (or reasonable grounds for such) is based.

- The whereabouts of the laundered property (if known) is passed as soon as is practicable to the MLRO.

- Additional information held by the individual that identifies other parties involved in or connected to the matter should also be given to the MLRO.

4.4   Failure to disclose

An offence is committed if an individual fails to make a report comprising the required disclosure as soon as is practicable either in the form of an:

- Internal report to his MLRO or

- A SAR to a person authorised by the National Crime Agency (NCA) to receive disclosures.

- The obligation to make the required disclosure arises when: a person knows or suspects, or has reasonable grounds for knowing or suspecting that another person is engaged in money laundering.

An MLRO is obliged to report to the NCA if he is satisfied that the information received in an internal report is serious in nature.

An MLRO may commit an offence if he fails to pass on reportable information in internal reports that he has received, as soon as is practicable, to NCA.

The maximum penalty for failure to disclose is 5 year imprisonment and/or an unlimited fine.

4.5   Exceptions to the duty to report

The obligation of an accountant to report does NOT apply if:

1   The information which forms the basis of knowledge or suspicion or the reasonable grounds to know or suspect was obtained other than in the course of the accountant's business, for example, on a social occasion

2   The information came about in privileged circumstances, that is in order for the accountant to provide legal advice, such as explaining a client's tax liability (except when it is judged that the advice has been sought to enable the client to commit a criminal offence or avoid detection) or expert opinion or services in relation to actual or contemplated legal proceedings

3   There is a reasonable excuse for not reporting, in which case the report must be made as soon as reasonable in the circumstances.

4.6   Protected and Authorised disclosures

Reports made under POCA are either protected disclosures or authorised disclosures.

Protected disclosure

Any report providing the required disclosure which is made by any person, not just an accountant, forming a money laundering suspicion, at work or when carrying out professional activities (whether or not providing accountancy services to clients), is a protected disclosure.

This means the person is protected against allegations of breach of confidentiality; however the restriction on disclosure of information was imposed.

Note: Any individual, business or organisation may make a voluntary protected disclosure; it is only in the regulated sector that such reports are compulsory.

Authorised disclosure

Any person who realises they may have engaged in or be about to engage in money laundering should make what is known as an authorised disclosure to the appropriate authority.

This may provide a defence against charges of money laundering provided it is made before the act is carried out (and NCA's consent to the act is obtained), or it is made as soon as possible on the initiative of that person after the act is done and with good reason being shown for the delay.

For example, the person did not realise that criminal property was involved and made the report on their own initiative as soon as this was suspected/known).

If NCA's consent is refused within seven working days, law enforcement has a further 31 calendar days (the 'moratorium period') to further the investigation into the reported matter and take further action e.g. restrain or seize funds.

If consent, or a refusal, is not received by the member within 7 working days, starting on the first working day after the consent request was made, consent is deemed.

If a refusal is received within that 7 working days, then the member may continue with the client relationship or transaction after a further 31 days has elapsed, starting with the day on which the member received notice of the refusal, unless a restraining order is obtained to prohibit this.

There is no deemed consent in relation to suspicions of terrorist financing.

 Test your understanding 4

Is the MLRO an internal or external person?

Is NCA is an internal or external body?

 Test your understanding 5

Tony is an accountant working for McIntosh Ltd.

Recently Meg plc, a customer of McIntosh Ltd, sent in a cheque for £100,000 in payment of an invoice for £20,000. When Tony queried this, the client said it was a mistake and asked for a cheque for the difference of £80,000 to be written to Omnivac plc, a sister company of Meg plc.

Advise Tony.

 Test your understanding 6

Emma is an accountant in practice working on the audit of Ghest Ltd.

During the audit Emma discovered that some customers of Ghest Ltd have overpaid their invoices and some have paid twice. On further investigation Emma discovers that the Ghest Ltd has a policy of retaining all overpayments by customers and crediting them to the profit and loss account if they are not claimed within a year.

Advise Emma.

Test your understanding 7

Jemma works as a trainee accountant within a firm of accountants. She is preparing a personal tax return for a client called Mr Derman.

To prepare the personal tax return Jemma requires information about Mr Derman's capital gains so she has been looking at the various share purchases and sales that Mr Derman has made through the tax year.

Jemma has become suspicious as she has noticed that Mr Derman only buys shares in small amounts of less than £100 at a time, but does several of these transactions a day and uses a number of different brokers through which he buys the shares.

Discuss whether or not Mr Derman has committed any offences and advise Jemma.

5 Tipping off

5.1 The offence of tipping off for accountants

Definition

Tipping off is the legal term meaning

- to tell the potential offender of money laundering that the necessary authorities have been informed, or

- to disclose anything that might prejudice an investigation.

Once an accountant has made a report, or has become aware that a report has been made, a criminal offence is committed if information is disclosed that is likely to prejudice any actual or contemplated investigation following the report.

The person making the disclosure does not have to intend to prejudice an investigation for this offence to apply.

Note: The report does not have to have been made by the person making the tip-off; that person merely needs to know or suspect that one has been made to a MLRO, NCA, HMRC or the police.

The maximum penalty for tipping off is five years imprisonment or an unlimited fine.

Tipping off is a serious criminal offence. You commit the offence if you make any disclosure likely to prejudice an investigation. An example might be if you tell the client that a SAR is or is about to be filed in respect of them. You don't have to speak to commit the offence. You can even tip off by failing to respond where an answer is expected.

There are exceptions that apply in certain circumstances, including those where a person does not know or suspect that the disclosure would prejudice a money laundering investigation, and where the disclosure is made in a valid attempt to persuade a client not to commit a money laundering offence.

Considerable care is required in carrying out any communications with clients or third parties following a report. Before any disclosure is made relating to matters referred to in an internal report or SAR, it is important to consider carefully whether or not it is likely to constitute offences of tipping off or prejudicing an investigation.

It is suggested that businesses keep records of these deliberations and the conclusions reached.

However, individuals and businesses in the regulated sector will frequently need to continue to deliver their professional services and a way needs to be found to achieve this without falling foul of the tipping off offence.

5.2 Prejudicing an investigation

An offence may be committed where **any** person (not just an accountant):

- knows or suspects that a money laundering investigation is being conducted or is about to be conducted; and

- makes a disclosure which is likely to prejudice the investigation; or

- falsifies, conceals or destroys documents relevant to the investigation, or causes that to happen.

The person making the disclosure does not have to intend to prejudice an investigation for this offence to apply.

However, there is a defence available if the person making the disclosure did not know or suspect the disclosure would be prejudicial, did not know or suspect the documents were relevant, or did not intend to conceal any facts from the person carrying out the investigation.

5.3 Record keeping

Under the MLR, records should be maintained to assist any future law enforcement investigation relating to clients, and to demonstrate that the accountant has complied with statutory obligations. Such records should include:

- copies of or reference to the Customer Due Diligence identification evidence (see below). These records must be kept for 5 years starting with the date on which the accountant's relationship with the client ends

- copies or originals of documents relating to transactions that have been subject to Customer Due Diligence measures or ongoing monitoring. These must be kept for 5 years starting with the date on which the accountant completed the client's instructions.

 Test your understanding 8

What is the maximum prison term for tipping off?

6 Customer Due Diligence

6.1 AAT ethics guidelines

When considering **any** new client engagement, the AAT member should assess the likelihood of money laundering.

6.2 When to apply Customer Due Diligence? (CDD)

CDD must be applied by accountants in practice to all clients **before** services are provided to them.

The one exception to this is where to do so would interrupt the normal conduct of business and there is little risk of money laundering or terrorist financing, in which case the accountant must always

- find out who the client claims to be before commencing the client's instructions and

- complete CDD as soon as reasonably possible afterwards.

Money laundering regulations state that CDD must be applied in the following situations:

- When establishing a business relationship.
- When carrying out an occasional transaction (i.e. involving €15,000 or the equivalent in sterling or more).
- Where there is a suspicion of money laundering or terrorist financing.
- Where there are doubts about previously obtained customer identification information.

6.3 Elements of Customer Due Diligence for new clients

There are three elements to CDD for new clients:

1 Find out who the client claims to be – name, address, and date of birth – and obtain evidence to check that the client is as claimed.

2 Obtain evidence so the accountant is satisfied that he or she knows who any beneficial owners are. This means beneficial owners must be considered on an individual basis. Generally, a beneficial owner is an individual who ultimately owns 25% or more of the client or the transaction property.

3 Obtain information on the purpose and intended nature of the transaction.

The evidence obtained can be documentary, data or information from a reliable and independent source, or a mix of all of these.

If CDD cannot be completed, **the accountant must not act for the client** – and should consider whether to submit an Internal Report or Suspicious Activity Report, as appropriate.

6.4 On-going monitoring of existing clients

On-going monitoring must be applied to existing clients. This means that an accountant must:

- Carry out appropriate and risk-sensitive CDD measures to any transaction which appears to be inconsistent with knowledge of the client or the client's business or risk profile.

    For example, if a client suddenly has an injection of significant funds, check the source of funds. If a beneficial owner is revealed, obtain evidence of the beneficial owner's identity and the nature and purpose of the injection of the funds.

- Keep CDD documents, data and information up to date.

    For example, if a client company has a change to its directorship, update records accordingly.

Test your understanding 9

A prospective new client comes to see you and asks you to invest £20,000 in cash into a business opportunity. However, he does not want to tell you his name or address.

Do you continue with the transaction?

7 Whistleblowing

7.1 The ethics of whistleblowing

Thousands of workers witness wrongdoing at work. Most remain silent. They decide that it is not their concern; that nothing they can do would improve things, or they cannot afford problems at work.

Other workers choose to speak out. They 'blow the whistle' on unethical and illegal conduct in the workplace.

 Definition

Whistleblowing means disclosing information that a worker believes is evidence of illegality, gross waste, gross mismanagement, abuse of power, or substantial and specific danger to the public health and safety.

Whistleblower actions may save lives, money, or the environment. However, instead of praise for the public service of 'committing the truth' whistleblowers are often targeted for retaliation, harassment, intimidation, demotion, dismissal and blacklisting.

 Example 3 – Whistleblowing

Tim, a civil engineer, believes that a certain building practice is unsafe and reports this to his employer. The employer does not act on the report so Tim takes it to his professional body. This body also does not act to Tim's satisfaction, so he then decides to take the report to the media. The employer dismisses Tim for gross misconduct in breaching confidentiality.

The ethics of whistleblowing highlights the matters that you should consider before you blow the whistle. It takes a realistic look at the effectiveness of the protection provided by the Public Interest Disclosure Act 1998.

7.2 Public Interest Disclosure Act (PIDA) 1998

Generally, as an employee, you owe a duty of loyalty to your employer as well as to the accountancy profession. However, there may be times where there is a conflict between the two.

For example, your manager may ask you to 'cook the books' to reduce the company's VAT liability. Although this is clearly wrong and you should not be involved in doing this, how do you resolve such a problem?

In this particular scenario, you would need to speak to your manager and advise him or her that you have concerns about doing this and cannot be involved in such an activity. If there is still a disagreement about a significant ethical issue with your manager, you should then raise the matter with higher levels of management or non-executive directors. Finally, if there is a material issue and you have exhausted all other avenues, you may wish to consider resigning – however, it is strongly recommended that you obtain legal advice before doing so.

In addition, you may decide to take the bolder step of external whistle blowing.

Note: The syllabus for EFTA includes both internal **and** external aspects of whistleblowing.

Where you have blown the whistle but decided not to resign, in certain circumstances you may be protected from dismissal by the Public Interest Disclosure Act 1998 (PIDA) where you disclose otherwise confidential information. The Act (which has also been referred to as 'the Whistleblowers' Charter') gives protection where you have made a 'qualifying disclosure' (i.e. disclosure of information which you reasonably believe shows that a criminal offence, breach of a legal obligation, miscarriage of justice, breach of health and safety legislation or environmental damage has occurred, is occurring or is likely to occur).

You need to show that you made the disclosure in good faith, reasonably believed that the information disclosed was true and that you would otherwise be victimised or the evidence concealed or destroyed; or that the concern has already been raised with the employer/external prescribed regulator (i.e. a body prescribed under PIDA such as Customs and Excise).

Test your understanding 10

Vincent, an accountant working in industry, discovered that the company he worked for was involved in illegal pollution and decided to leak this information anonymously to the press.

A month later Vincent's department was closed down and Vincent made redundant. Vincent is now claiming that he has been victimised because he was a whistleblower and is seeking protection under PIDA.

Comment on Vincent's case.

8 Summary

This chapter has introduced you to some very important legislation.

It is vital you are able to both recite and apply the money laundering regulation in order to progress through this assessment.

Make sure you know what the definitions are!

9 Test your understanding answers

Test your understanding 1

A farmer is exposed to the following risks (any FOUR required):

- Adverse weather conditions affecting a harvest of crops.
- Sickness affecting livestock.
- Theft of farm equipment.
- Competition from imported goods.
- Pressure from supermarkets to reduce prices.
- Changes in customer taste.

Test your understanding 2

D

Reputational risk.

Test your understanding 3

A

Balance of probabilities.

Test your understanding 4

The MLRO is an **internal** person.

The NCA is an **external** body.

KAPLAN PUBLISHING

Test your understanding 5

The overpayment and request to pay a third party are grounds for suspicion of money laundering (see note below).

Any overpayment by a customer should be thoroughly investigated by a senior member of finance function staff and only repaid to the customer once it has been established that it is right/legal to do so.

Similarly the request to pay a third party should be scrutinised before any payment is agreed to. Without further information the transaction does not make commercial sense.

Unless investigations satisfy any concerns raised, then

- Tom should report the matter to the firm's MRLO.

- McIntosh Ltd should refuse the payment.

- The MRLO should fill in a Suspicious Activity Report (SAR) to be sent to NCA.

Tutorial note: It seems highly unlikely a customer would overpay by £80,000 by accident! Also, why doesn't the client, Meg plc, simply want McIntosh Ltd to repay them and then it up to them whether they want to pay anything to Omnivac plc? Is it to make funds difficult to trace, so 'dirty' cash becomes a nice 'clean' cheque from a reputable accounting firm?

Test your understanding 6

Emma should consider whether the retention of the overpayments might amount to theft by Ghest Ltd from its customers. If so, the client will be in possession of the proceeds of its crime, a money laundering offence.

In the case of minor irregularities where there is nothing to suggest dishonest behaviour, (for example where Ghest Ltd attempted to return the overpayments to its customers, or if the overpayments were mistakenly overlooked), Emma may be satisfied that no criminal property is involved and therefore a report is not required.

If there are no such indications that Ghest Ltd has acted honestly, Emma should conclude that Ghest Ltd may have acted dishonestly.

Emma must thus make a report to her firm's MLRO.

Test your understanding 7

In this example it is probably the case that Mr Derman is a harmless eccentric who chooses to buy shares in small amounts or is indecisive, so often buys some shares only to buy more soon after.

On the other hand it may be that Mr Derman buys shares in small amounts and then sells them to disguise the source of his funds and make the proceeds from the sale of shares appear to be more legitimate. In that case he would have hidden the original source of the money. The use of different brokers to carry out the same activities could indicate that he does not wish to cause suspicion by one large transaction.

As Jemma works for a firm of accountants, she is required to make a disclosure to her firm's nominated money laundering reporting officer if she suspects money laundering. It is up to the MLRO to decide whether Jemma has been 'over-enthusiastic' and that the situation is harmless or if there are genuine grounds for taking the matter further.

Test your understanding 8

The maximum prison term for tipping off is 5 years.

Test your understanding 9

You would be unable to complete a due diligence report on this potential customer, there you should not continue with the transaction.

Also the way in which you have been approached could be grounds for suspicious activity. It would be appropriate to report the dealings on the MLRO if possible, if not to NCA.

Test your understanding 10

To gain protection from PIDA, Vincent would have to demonstrate that he was made redundant because he was a whistleblower.

In this case that would be very difficult as he made his disclosure anonymously.

10 Additional Test your understanding questions

Test your understanding 11

Adam, an AAT member within the UK, works for a firm of accountants. Adam has found an error in a client's tax affairs. The client has refused to disclose this known error, after Adam has given notice of this error and an appropriate amount of time has been allowed to take action.

Which of the following is Adam obliged to report this refusal to and the information surrounding it:

A   HM Revenue and Customs (HMRC)

B   The Money Laundering Reporting Officer (MLRO)

C   The National Crime Agency (NCA)

Test your understanding 12

(a)   If you suspect money laundering is occurring, you should

    A   Talk it through with the people involved, to confirm that you have understood the situation fully.

    B   Report the problem to your line manager.

    C   Disclose the issue to your MLRO.

(b)   If you are involved in money laundering, you face

    A   Life imprisonment.

    B   Public flogging.

    C   14 years imprisonment, and/or an unlimited fine.

Test your understanding 13

Fabio has recently discovered that his company has been fly tipping waste rather than paying to dispose of it correctly.

Answer the following questions by selecting the appropriate option.

(a)   If Fabio reports the issue to the relevant authorities, he is protected from dismissal by the

     A   Disability Discrimination Act 2006

     B   Public Interest Disclosure Act 1998

     C   Companies Act 2006

(b)   The actions of his company are an example of

     A   Abuse of power

     B   Gross mismanagement

     C   Illegality

 Test your understanding 14

David, a member in practice has been approached by a potential new client.

Answer the following question by selecting the TWO appropriate options.

As part of his customer due diligence process, which of the following actions must David undertake?

- Verify the client's identity on the basis of documents, data or other reliable information.

- Verify the value of the client's assets and liabilities.

- Obtain information on the purpose and intended nature of the client relationship.

- Notify the AAT.

Test your understanding 15

(a) Customer due diligence refers to:

   A   Making sure that your client is hard working

   B   Verifying your client's identity

   C   Checking that your client will pay his bills

(b) Customer Due Diligence is performed to comply with:

   A   Companies Act 2006

   B   Money laundering legislation

   C   AAT ethical guidance

11 Additional Test your understanding answers

 Test your understanding 11

B

The Money Laundering Reporting Officer (MLRO).

 Test your understanding 12

(a)   **C** – If you suspect money laundering is occurring, you should disclose the issue to your MLRO.

(b)   **C** – If you are involved in money laundering, you face 14 years imprisonment, and/or an unlimited fine.

 Test your understanding 13

(a)   **B** – If Fabio reports the issue to the relevant authorities, he is protected from dismissal by the Public Interest Disclosure Act 1998.

(b)   **C** – The actions of his company are an example of Illegality.

 Test your understanding 14

As part of his customer due diligence process, David must undertake the following:

- Verify the client's identity on the basis of documents, data or other reliable information.

- Obtain information on the purpose and intended nature of the client relationship.

Test your understanding 15

(a) **B** – Customer due diligence refers to Verifying your client's identity.

(b) **B** – Customer due diligence is performed to comply with Money laundering legislation.

Legal considerations – II

Introduction

Accountants in the workplace can be exposed to many risks, for example money laundering, as seen in the previous chapter. However this chapter details further areas such as bribery and fraud.

Accountants must be vigilant to safeguard themselves and the businesses they work for against this.

ASSESSMENT CRITERIA
1.1 Explain why it is important to act ethically
1.2 Explain how to act ethically
2.3 Explain the importance of objectivity
2.4 Explain the importance of behaving professionally
2.5 Explain the importance of being competent and acting with due care
2.6 Explain the importance of confidentiality and when confidential information may be disclosed.
4.2 Identify the relevant body to which questionable behaviour must be reported

CONTENTS
1 Bribery
2 Fraud
3 Data protection
4 Other legal and regulatory requirements

1 Bribery

1.1 Bribery

As well as ensuring they are not involved in bribery personally, accountants should be vigilant to identify situations when their firm (or clients) are involved in or exposed to bribery.

Example 1 – Bribery

Bribery is now recognized to be one of the world's greatest challenges.

For example, KPMG surveyed FTSE 100 companies in August 2009 and found that two thirds said it was not possible to do business in some countries without being involved in bribery, yet only 35 per cent had stopped doing business there.

Test your understanding 1

Give some reasons why businesses should not be engaged in bribery.

Accountants need to very careful when deciding whether to accept gifts, hospitality and inducements, especially if 'excessive', as these may be perceived to be bribes.

Bribery can be viewed as a threat to objectivity and also compromises the fundamental principles of integrity and professional behaviour.

1.2 The Bribery Act (2010)

The Bribery Act (2010) creates the following offences:

1   Bribing a person to induce or reward them to perform a relevant function improperly (active bribery).

2   Requesting, accepting or receiving a bribe as a reward for performing a relevant function improperly (passive bribery).

3   Using a bribe to influence a foreign official to gain a business advantage.

4   Failing to prevent bribery on behalf of a commercial organisation.

Example 2 – Hospitality or bribery?

Firms are allowed to provide hospitality.

For example, to provide tickets to sporting events, take clients to dinner or offer gifts to clients as a reflection of good relations.

However where hospitality may be a cover for bribing someone, the authorities would look at such things as the level of hospitality offered, the way in which it was provided and the level of influence the person receiving it had on the business decision in question.

 Example 3 – Facilitation payments

Facilitation payments are additional payments to induce officials to perform routine functions they are otherwise obliged to perform.

For example, additional payments to customs officials so they prioritise processing the import of your goods.

The UK Act criminalises facilitation payments abroad. Other countries, such as the United States, do not prohibit such payments abroad.

Note: You can pay for legally required administrative fees or 'fast-track' services. These are not facilitation payments.

1.3 Penalty and culpability

Under the Bribery Act (2010), imprisonment for up to ten years with unlimited fine.

Companies can be liable for bribery committed for their benefit by their employees or other associated persons.

A company or corporate entity is culpable for board-level complicity in bribery, including bribery through intermediaries. There is also personal liability for senior company officers that turn a blind eye to such board-level bribery.

In addition, a company or corporate entity is culpable for bribes given to a third party with the intention of obtaining or retaining business for the organisation or obtaining or retaining an advantage useful to the conduct of the business by their employees and associated persons, even if they had no knowledge of those actions.

1.4 Defences

The Act is unusual in that a business can be guilty of an offence if an employee or associate commits an offence even if the management are not aware of, or condoned, the unlawful behaviour.

Because of this KPMG have described the Act as 'one of the most draconian pieces of anti-bribery and corruption (AB&C) legislation in the world'.

If prosecuted under the act, then the company can invoke in its defence only that it 'had in place **adequate** procedures designed to prevent persons associated [with the company] from undertaking such conduct'.

1.5 Jurisdiction and application

The scope of the law is extra-territorial. Under the Bribery Act, a relevant person or company can be prosecuted for the above crimes if the crimes are committed abroad.

The Bribery Act applies to UK citizens, residents and companies established under UK law. In addition, non-UK companies can be held liable for a failure to prevent bribery if they do business in the UK.

 Test your understanding 2

A UK client company is considering expanding its business into a new country.

Describe some preliminary steps the company could undertake to assess the risks of bribery and corruption in the country.

 Test your understanding 3

FGH plc, a UK company, manufactures laboratory equipment. Last year FGH plc won a major government contract in Country X to supply equipment to all state-run universities and hospitals.

However, it has since come to light that Mrs Li, the agent representing FGH in Country X, treated government ministers to expensive holidays and gifts as part of the bidding process. The Board of FGH claim no knowledge of such gifts and are adamant they didn't authorise this.

Discuss whether FGH could be guilty of an offence under the UK Bribery Act 2010.

2 **Fraud**

2.1 What is fraud?

 Definition

Fraud is an intentional act involving the use of deception to obtain an unjust or illegal advantage – essentially 'theft by deception'.

Fraud (intentional) should be contrasted with error (unintentional).

Example 4 – Fraud or error

If a purchase ledger clerk deliberately enters a false invoice from a friend into the purchase ledger, hoping that it will be paid so that the clerk and the friend can split the proceeds, this is a fraud. However if the clerk accidentally enters an invoice twice into the ledger, this is an error.

Note that fraud may be carried out by management, employees or third parties. For example:

- Managers may deliberately select inappropriate accounting policies.

- Employees may steal the proceeds of cash sales and omit to enter the sale into the accounting records.

- Third parties may send bogus invoices to the company, hoping that they will be paid in error.

Fraud is a criminal offence, punishable by a fine or imprisonment.

 Test your understanding 4

A safety inspector has found several safety violations in the manufacturing plant where you work. Correcting these will cost £30,000.

The inspector has offered to ignore the violations in return for a secret payment of £5,000, which your boss has asked you to organise. The workers will never be told about the safety violations and the inspector will file a report stating that the plant passes all the safety regulations.

What would you do?

2.2 Different types of fraud

Examples of fraud include:

- Crimes against consumers or clients, e.g. Misrepresenting the quality of goods; pyramid trading schemes; selling counterfeit goods.

- Employee crimes against employers, e.g. Payroll fraud; falsifying expense claims; theft of cash.

- Crimes against investors, consumers and employees, e.g. Financial statement fraud.

- Crimes against financial institutions, e.g. Using lost and stolen credit cards; fraudulent insurance claims.

- Crimes against government, e.g. Social security benefit claims fraud; tax evasion.

- Crimes by professional criminals, e.g. Money laundering; advance fee fraud.

- E-crime by people using computers, e.g. Spamming; Copyright crimes; hacking.

2.3 The Fraud Act (2006)

Fraud is a criminal act and can be broken down into three distinct offences

- **Fraud by false representation**

  Is defined by Section 2 of the Act as a case where a person makes 'any representation as to fact or law ... express or implied' which they know to be untrue or misleading.

- **Fraud by failing to disclose information**

  Is defined by Section 3 of the Act as a case where a person fails to disclose any information to a third party when they are under a legal duty to disclose such information.

- **Fraud by abuse of position**

  Is defined by Section 4 of the Act as a case where a person occupies a position where they are expected to safeguard the financial interests of another person, and abuses that position.

In all three classes of fraud, it requires that for an offence to have occurred, the person must have acted dishonestly, and that they had to have acted with the intent of making a gain for themselves or anyone else, or inflicting a loss (or a risk of loss) on another.

2.4 Fraud prevention

The aim of preventative controls is to reduce opportunity and remove temptation from potential offenders. Prevention techniques include the introduction of policies, procedures and controls, and activities such as training and fraud awareness to stop fraud from occurring.

The existence of a fraud strategy is itself a deterrent. This can be achieved through:

- **An anti-fraud culture**

    Where minor unethical practices are overlooked, for example, expenses or time recording, this may lead to a culture in which larger frauds occur. High ethical standards bring long term benefits as customers, suppliers, employees and the community realise they are dealing with a trustworthy organisation.

- **Risk awareness**

    Fraud should never be discounted, and there should be awareness among all staff that there is always the possibility that fraud is taking place. It is important to raise awareness through training programmes. Particular attention should be given to training and awareness among those people involved in receiving cash, purchasing and paying suppliers.

    Publicity can also be given to fraud that has been exposed. This serves as a reminder to those who may be tempted to commit fraud and a warning to those responsible for the management of controls.

- **Whistleblowing**

    Fraud may be suspected by those who are not personally involved. People must be encouraged to raise the alarm about fraud.

- **Sound internal control systems**

    Sound systems of internal control should monitor fraud by identifying risks and then putting into place procedures to monitor and report on those risks.

2.5 Fraud detection

A common misbelieve is that external auditors find fraud. This is actually rarely the case. Their letters of engagement typically state that it is not their responsibility to look for fraud.

Most frauds are discovered accidentally, or as a result of information received (whistleblowing).

Some methods of discovering fraud are:

- **Performing regular checks**

  For example stocktaking and cash counts.

- **Warning signals**

  For example:

  - Failures in internal control procedures.
  - Lack of information provided to auditors.
  - Unusual behaviour by individual staff members.
  - Accounting difficulties.
  - Whistleblowers.

2.6 Fraud response

The fraud response plan sets out the arrangements for dealing with suspected cases of fraud, theft or corruption.

- It provides procedures for evidence gathering that will enable decision-making and that will subsequently be admissible in any legal action.

- The fraud response plan also has a deterrent value and can help to restrict damage and minimise losses to the organisation.

- Internal disciplinary action, in accordance with personnel policies.

- Civil litigation for recovery of loss.

- Criminal prosecution through the police.

Within the response plan responsibilities should be allocated to:

- Managers, who should take responsibility for detecting fraud in their area.

- Finance Director, who has overall responsibility for the organisational response to fraud including the investigation. This role may be delegated to a fraud officer or internal security officer.

- Personnel (Human Resources department), who will have responsibility for disciplinary procedures and issues of employment law and practice.

- Audit committee, who should review the details of all frauds and receive reports of any significant events.

- Internal auditors, who will most likely have the task of investigating the fraud.

- External auditors, to obtain expertise.

- Legal advisors, in relation to internal disciplinary, civil or criminal responses.

- Public Relations, in case the fraud is so significantly large that it will come to public attention.

- Police, where it is policy to prosecute all those suspected of fraud.

- Insurers, where there is likely to be a claim.

2.7 Theft

According to the Theft Act 1968, someone is guilty of theft if he/she 'dishonestly appropriates property belonging to another with the intention of permanently depriving them of it'.

Accountants hold client monies on trust and anyone who mishandles client monies may be guilty of theft as well as fraud.

2.8 Employee malfeasance risk

You may come across the term 'malfeasance'. Malfeasance means doing wrong or committing an offence, so employee malfeasance risk refers to organisations' exposure to risks of actions by employees that result in an offence or crime. While this can include fraud and theft, the term includes other offences as well.

Examples of employee malfeasance are:

- Fraud and theft, including making false expenses claims

- Inappropriate use of computer systems

- Illegal dumping of waste.

 Test your understanding 5

Matilda is a professional accountant in practice. A client recently gave her £2,500 in order to be able to pay the client's tax bill when it falls due.

(a) In what legal capacity does Matilda hold the money?

(b) If Matilda takes some of the money for her own use, what crime(s) is she guilty of?

3 Data protection

3.1 The Data Protection Act (1998)

The Data Protection Act gives individuals the right to know what information is held about them. It provides a framework to ensure that personal information is handled properly.

The Act works in two ways.

- Firstly, it gives rules and principles concerning the use of data.

- Secondly, it provides individuals with important rights concerning data held about them.

There are, however, exemptions to the Data Protection Act. For example:

- Any personal data that is held by MI5 and MI6 for a national security reason is not covered.

- Personal data held for domestic purposes only at home does not have to keep to the rules – e.g. a list of your friends' addresses.

3.2 Data protection principles

Subject to certain exemptions, anyone who processes personal information must ensure that:

- Data should be processed fairly and lawfully.

- Data should be obtained only for specified and lawful purposes.

- Data should be adequate, relevant and not excessive.

- Data should be accurate and, where necessary, kept up to date.

- Data should not be kept longer than is necessary.

- Data should be processed in accordance with your rights.

- Data should be kept secure.

- Data should not be transferred to other countries without adequate protection.

3.3 Rights concerning information

The second area covered by the Act provides individuals with important rights, including the right to find out what personal information is held on computer and most paper records, on payment of a reasonable fee.

Should an individual or organisation feel they're being denied access to personal information they're entitled to, or feel their information has not been handled according to the eight principles, they can contact the Information Commissioner's Office for help.

Complaints are usually dealt with informally, but if this isn't possible, enforcement action can be taken.

3.4 Registration

Subject to certain exemptions, all users of computers who are intending to hold personal data are required to register and supply the following details:

- Name and address of data user.

- Description of, and purpose for which, data is held.

- Description of source data.

- Identification of persons to whom it is disclosed.

- Names and non-UK countries to which transmission is desired.

- Name of persons responsible for dealing with data subject enquiries.

- If an organisation fails to register, this is a criminal offence, although compensation is through a civil action.

3.5 The Information Commissioner's Office (ICO)

The ICO maintains a public register of data controllers.

If any part of the data controller's register becomes inaccurate, then they should notify the ICO within 28 days. If an organisation fails to register, this is a **criminal offence**, although compensation is through a civil action.

 Test your understanding 6

Are the following statements true or false?

1   We can only process data with the consent of the data subject.

2   It's illegal to process data unless the processing is covered by our notification with the Information Commissioner.

3   The Data Protection Act prevents us from holding duplicate copies of data.

4   If data is no longer needed for the purposes for which it was gathered, it must be destroyed.

4 Other legal and regulatory requirements

An awareness of the following additional legal and regulatory requirements that may affect your work within the accountancy profession is required.

4.1 Insider trading

On the basis of inside information, it is against the law to buy or sell shares or pass on, tip or disclose material, non-public information to others outside the company including family and friends.

While working for your company, you may learn important and confidential information, called 'inside information' about your company, or about one of your company's suppliers, customers or business partners, which could affect the company's share price.

Examples of information that may be considered material, non-public information in some circumstances are:

- A substantial contract award or termination that has not been publicly disclosed

- The gain or loss of a significant customer that has not been publicly disclosed

- Undisclosed negotiations and agreements regarding mergers, concessions, joint ventures, divestments, etc.

- Undisclosed financial results or changes in earnings projections

- Undisclosed management changes

- Information that is considered confidential.

Even when material information has been publicly disclosed, each insider must continue to refrain from buying or selling the shares in question until the beginning of the third business day after the information has been publicly released, to allow the markets time to absorb the information.

4.2 Health and safety legislation

There are a number of potential hazards in any workplace, including:

- Unsafe electrics

- Torn carpets

- Poor lighting

- Wet floors

- Top heavy filing cabinets.

The law typically puts the responsibility for health and safety on both the employer and the employee.

The employer has a duty, amongst other things, to

- provide a safe working environment

- prevent risks to health

- ensure that plant and machinery is safe to use and that safe working practices are set up and followed

- inform staff of any potential hazards

- provide adequate first aid facilities

- check that the right equipment is used and that is regularly maintained

- set up emergency plans.

If employers fail to provide a safe and healthy working environment, they may be in breach of common law, enabling employees to make a civil claim against them.

In addition, they may be guilty of a criminal offence and be open to prosecution.

The employee has, amongst other things, a duty to

- take reasonable care of their own health and safety

- take reasonable care not to put other people at risk

- cooperate with their employer to ensure they have adequate training and are familiar with their employer's health and safety policies

- report any injuries suffered as a result of performing their job

- inform their employer if anything affects their ability to work safely.

4.3 Employment protection and equality law

The law has given employees and in many cases other workers who might not count as employee's rights and entitlements in relation to:

- how they are disciplined and dismissed

- how their grievances are handled, wages, absence from work and sickness, holidays, work breaks and working hours, time off for family emergencies

- maternity and paternity leave, the right to apply for flexible working, redundancy and retirement.

All workers have the right not to be discriminated against in relation to their gender or orientation, race, age, disabilities, or religion and beliefs.

Staff who feel they have been denied their rights have redress by taking their employers to an Employment Tribunal.

The primary legislation safeguarding these rights is the **Equality Act (2010)**. The primary purpose of this act was to consolidate the complicated and numerous array of Acts and Regulations, which formed the basis of anti-discrimination law in Great Britain.

Example 5 – Discrimination

There are three types of discrimination that an equal opportunities policy will attempt to prevent:

- **Direct discrimination** – this occurs when an employer treats an employee less favourably than another, due to their gender, race, etc. For example, if a driving job was only open to male applicants.

  This may be allowed by law in certain, tightly defined, circumstances.

- **Indirect discrimination** – this occurs when a working condition or rule disadvantages one group of people more than another. For instance, a requirement for male employees to be clean-shaven would put some religious groups at a disadvantage.

  Indirect discrimination is often illegal, unless it is necessary for the working of the business and there is no way round it.

- **Victimisation** – this means an employer treating an employee less favourably because they have made, or tried to make, a complaint about discrimination.

Test your understanding 7

A female employee is frequently subject to rude jokes of a sexual nature made by her male colleagues and comments about her weight and appearance. The woman finds this offensive and hurtful however her colleagues tell her that they don't mean anything by their comments and it is just friendly banter.

What type of discrimination is the female employee subject to?

A   Direct discrimination

B   Indirect discrimination

C   Victimisation

D   Sexual harassment

5 Summary

This chapter includes essential elements of the Ethics for Accountants syllabus.

The understanding of the UK Bribery Act and fraud in particular are all required within the assessment criteria, and are regularly examined areas.

Due to the nature of the business of accountants in practice have to deal with these issues within their working lives.

6 Test your understanding answers

Test your understanding 1

Why bribery is wrong – the ethical argument

- It is a misuse of power and position and has a disproportionate impact on the poor and disadvantaged.

- It undermines the integrity of all involved and damages the fabric of the organizations to which they belong.

Why bribery is wrong – the business argument

- Legal risks – bribery may be illegal

- Reputational risks if found out

- Financial costs – fines and the cost of bribes

- Pressure to repeat offend/exposure to blackmail

- Impact on staff – trust and confidence eroded.

Test your understanding 2

- Use simple internet searches to find out about the levels of bribery in the particular country you propose to do business in.

- Consult the Foreign Office for advice.

- Consult business representative bodies here and in the relevant country for up to date local knowledge.

- UK firms can use the Government sponsored Business Anti-Corruption Portal aimed at small and medium sized businesses involved in overseas trade.

Test your understanding 3

The Bribery Act 2010 contains four offences:

1   bribing a person to induce or reward them to perform a relevant function improperly

2   requesting, accepting or receiving a bribe as a reward for performing a relevant function improperly

3   using a bribe to influence a foreign official to gain a business advantage

4   failing to prevent bribery on behalf of a commercial organisation.

Certainly the excessive nature of the hospitality would mean that it would be viewed as an attempt to bribe the MPs concerned to win the contract.

While FGH plc could argue that they are not guilty of 1, 2 and 3 above, they are likely to be found guilty under offence 4. Even though Mrs Li was an agent and not an employee, and even though the Board claim ignorance, the company could still be found guilty of failing to prevent bribery.

The only possible defence would be to demonstrate that they had adequate procedures in place to prevent bribery.

 ## Test your understanding 4

You should refuse to accept the £5,000 and report the actions of the safety inspector to the relevant authorities.

 ## Test your understanding 5

(a)   In trust/as a trustee.

(b)   Theft and/or fraud by abuse of position.

Test your understanding 6

1   False. While consent is usually desirable, it's not absolutely essential – there are many situations where processing without consent is 'fair and lawful', although firms do have a general obligation to inform individuals (as far as is practicable) how their data will be processed, when we gather the data.

2   True, as far as processing which we are required to notify is concerned.

3   False. However, unnecessary duplication will make it more difficult to meet the requirements of the DPA, as each copy has to be managed in accordance with the DPA.

4   True, in most cases. However, personal data can be retained indefinitely if it's being used for research purposes (including preservation as historical archives).

 Test your understanding 7

D

Sexual harassment is unwanted conduct of a sexual nature.

7 Additional Test your understanding questions

 Test your understanding 8

Tariq works for an electrical company called Techsafety Ltd. Tariq's role involves attending newly constructed office buildings and signing off on the safety of electrical work by providing an electrical certificate.

In March, Tariq attends a job at an office building. The construction time overran by a couple of months and the site manager, Tony, is now desperate for the electrical certificate. During his visit Tariq identified a few issues that still need looking at. Tony has offered to pay for Tariq and his family to have an all-expenses paid holiday during the summer holidays if Tariq can give him the certificate by the end of the day.

Analyse the situation from the perspective of the law relating to bribery. In particular explain which criminal offences may have been committed by the various parties.

Test your understanding 9

Answer the following questions by selecting the appropriate option in each case.

(a) Which of the following statements is true?

    A   Fraud is an honest mistake.

    B   Error is deliberate falsification.

    C   Fraud is committed with intent.

(b) Fraud risk is governed by:

    A   How much trouble you will get into if your boss finds out.

    B   How the press will report the fraud.

    C   Probability of fraud × size of resultant loss.

(c) Which of the flowing is the most effective method of dealing with fraud?

    A   Fraud prevention.

    B   Fraud detection.

Test your understanding 10

Which of the following types of new legislation would provide greater employment opportunities in large companies?

A   New laws on health and safety.

B   New laws to prevent discrimination in the workplace.

C   New laws making it more difficult to dismiss employees unfairly.

D   New laws on higher compensation for employer breaches of employment contracts.

 Test your understanding 11

Which of the following should be considered first in order to establish an effective internal control system that will minimise the likelihood of fraud?

A   Recruitment policy and checks on new personnel.

B   Identification of areas of potential risk.

C   Devising appropriate sanctions for inappropriate behaviour.

D   Segregation of duties in critical areas.

Test your understanding 12

A rogue trader has sent your company a bogus invoice for advertising in a non-existent publication.

The rogue spoke to a purchase ledger clerk at your company and convinced her that your company had placed several previous advertisements in the publication in the past, so that this repeat advertisement was genuine.

The clerk was innocently fooled into passing the invoice for payment.

(a)   Has the rogue committed a fraud?

(b)   Has the clerk committed a fraud?

(c)   Will the rogue be paid?

8 Additional Test your understanding answers

 Test your understanding 8

The Bribery Act 2010 creates four offences.

1 Bribing a person to induce or reward them to perform a relevant function improperly

2 Requesting, accepting or receiving a bribe as a reward for performing a relevant function improperly

3 Using a bribe to influence a foreign official to gain a business advantage

4 Failing to prevent bribery on behalf of a commercial organisation.

Applying the general law to the scenario, one can conclude as follows:

Tony is guilty of bribery under the Act (offence 1 above) as he is bribing Tariq by offering him a free family holiday in return for him issuing an electrical certificate.

If Tariq accepts the bribe and issues the certificate he will be guilty of receiving a bribe from Tony under the Act (offence 2 above).

Techsafety Ltd could also be guilty of bribery under the Act for failing to prevent bribery (offence 4 above) unless they can show that they had in place 'adequate procedures'.

 Test your understanding 9

(a) **C** – Fraud is committed with intent.

(b) **C** – Fraud risk = probability of fraud × size of resultant loss.

(c) **A** – The most effective method of dealing with fraud is fraud prevention.

Test your understanding 10

B

Equal opportunity policies widen opportunity and enlarge the potential pool of employees to recruit from. The other options, either indirectly or directly, reduce the potential for staff turnover and therefore limit the number of job vacancies available at any point in time.

 Test your understanding 11

B

Before fraud can be prevented it is first necessary to identify areas where fraud is likely to occur before preventative measures can be taken.

Test your understanding 12

(a) Yes. He is deliberately deceiving the company, hoping to be paid an amount of money.

(b) No. She has no dishonest intent, but has made a mistake in believing the rogue.

(c) It depends on the other controls in force. If the company has no other controls over payments apart from the clerk's authorisation, then the rogue will be paid. Hopefully there are other controls (e.g. supervisory controls) that will prevent any payment being made in such an instance.

KAPLAN PUBLISHING

The accountant in practice

5

Introduction

In this chapter we look at the guidelines applicable to members in practice covering accepting work through to earning a fair reward for the services rendered.

We also look at examples of unethical client behaviour and how to respond, with particular emphasis on confidentiality.

ASSESSMENT CRITERIA

1.1 Explain why it is important to act ethically

1.2 Explain how to act ethically

1.3 Explain the importance of values, culture and codes of practice/conduct

2.1 Explain the ethical code's conceptual framework of principles, threats, safeguards and professional judgement

2.3 Explain the importance of objectivity

3.1 Distinguish between ethical and unethical behaviour

3.2 Analyse a situation using the conceptual framework and the conflict resolution process

3.3 Develop an ethical course of action

3.4 Justify an appropriate action when requested to perform tasks that are beyond current experience or expertise

4.3 Report suspected money laundering in accordance with the regulations

CONTENTS

1 Accepting work

2 Tax services

3 Handling client monies

4 Client confidentiality revisited

5 Other considerations

6 Procedural aspects of new appointments

1 Accepting work

1.1 Fundamental principles and safeguards

Before accepting a new client relationship, a member in practice shall determine whether acceptance would create any threats to compliance with the fundamental principles.

Potential threats may be created by the characteristics and character of the client, or the nature of the client's business.

Examples of such threats include:

- The client's involvement in illegal activities (such as money laundering).

- Dishonesty.

- Questionable financial reporting practices.

A member in practice shall evaluate the significance of any threats and if they are not clearly insignificant, safeguards shall be determined and applied as necessary to eliminate them or reduce them to an acceptable level.

Examples of safeguards include:

- Obtaining knowledge and understanding of the client, its owners, managers and those responsible for its governance.

- Securing the client's commitment to improve corporate governance practices or internal controls.

- Ensuring that any concerns are addressed by way of a letter of engagement.

1.2 The need for competence

A member in practice shall agree to provide only those services that they are competent to perform.

A self-interest threat to professional competence and due care is created if the engagement team does not possess, or cannot acquire, the competencies necessary to properly carry out the engagement.

It is essential therefore for the profession in general and in the interests of their clients that accountants be encouraged to obtain advice when appropriate from those who are competent to provide it.

When a member in practice intends to rely on the advice or work of an expert, the member in practice shall determine whether such reliance is warranted. The member in practice shall consider factors such as reputation, expertise, resources available and applicable professional and ethical standards.

1.3 The need for objectivity

A member must not allow bias, conflict of interest or undue influence of others to override professional or business judgements.

These can include personal self-interest threats and other conflicts of interest.

Personal threats to independence

Self-interest threats to independence can arise when

- Holding a financial interest in a client, such as owning shares
- Having undue dependence on total fees from a client
- Receiving excessive hospitality and gifts from a client.

Similarly familiarity threats to independence can arise when

- Having a close business relationship with a client
- Having personal and family relationships with a client.

Conflicts of interest

Threats to objectivity due to conflict of interest may be created when

- A member in practice competes directly with a client.
- A member in practice has a joint venture with a major competitor of a client.
- A member in practice performs services for clients whose interests are in conflict.
- A member in practice performs services for clients who are in dispute with each other in relation to the matter or transaction in question.

 Test your understanding 1

Peter, an AAT member, has been asked by a friend to complete his tax self-assessment form for him. Unfortunately, Peter has never completed such a return before.

Potentially, which fundamental principle is threatened?

Test your understanding 2

Helen, an AAT member in practice at Integrity LLP, has been offered a job by one of her audit clients.

In order to maintain her independence, what course of action should Helen take?

- Resign immediately.

- Inform the partners at Integrity LLP and be removed from the audit of the client.

- Nothing – it is just an offer.

1.4 Professional liability

The risks inherent in an accountancy practice vary with the type of work undertaken. Some of this work may expose the member to the risk of a claim for damages due to his or her alleged negligence in the performance of it.

Negligence in this case means some act or omission that occurs because the member concerned has failed to exercise the degree of reasonable care and skill that is reasonably expected of him or her in the circumstances of that case resulting in financial loss to a person to whom a duty of care is owed.

Opinions expressed or advice given will generally not give rise to liability merely because in the light of later events they prove to have been wrong, even if they amounted to an error in judgement, provided they were arrived at using the care and skill that was reasonable for an accountant undertaking such work.

A member may and usually will be liable to his client for negligence not only in contract but also from other causes e.g. criminal acts, breaches of trust or breaches of contract.

He or she will also be liable for negligence to a third party to whom a duty of care was owed and who has suffered a loss as a result of the member's negligence.

It is not possible either in law or in fact to guard against every circumstance in which a member may risk incurring liability for professional negligence. When entering into contracts with clients, where there appears to be any doubt about the extent of the member's liability, the member is recommended to seek legal advice.

However, as discussed below, there are a number of steps that members can take to assist them in managing their liability.

- **Identifying the terms of the engagement**

   Before carrying out any work for a client a member should ensure that the exact duties to be performed and in particular any significant matters to be excluded.

- **Defining the specific tasks to be undertaken**

   A member should make clear in the letter of engagement the extent of the responsibilities he or she agrees to undertake, making particular reference to any information supplied by the client and relied on as a basis for the work, for which the client or others are responsible.

   Members should guard against the situation where they undertake to perform particular tasks, then during the course of the work find that it is impossible or unnecessary to perform all the tasks originally envisaged but do not agree with the client the change in the scope of the work.

- **Defining the responsibilities to be undertaken by the client**

   A member should make it clear in the engagement letter where responsibilities are to be undertaken by the client.

   For example, the client could reasonably be expected to check reports prepared by the member for completeness or accuracy before any use is made of it involving third parties.

- **Specifying any limitations on the work to be undertaken**

   In giving informal advice at the request of a client, or advice which must necessarily be based on incomplete information, a member should make it clear that such advice is subject to limitations and that consideration in depth may lead to a revision of the advice given.

- **Liability disclaimers**

   A member may find it advantageous to include in documents a clause disclaiming liability.

   Such a clause cannot however be relied on in all circumstances. For example, a court might hold that such a disclaimer represented an unreasonable exclusion of liability.

- **Professional Indemnity Insurance**

   All members in practice need to maintain an adequate level of Professional Indemnity Insurance cover.

   Professional Indemnity Insurance is also strongly recommended for student members who undertake self-employed work.

Test your understanding 3

Guthrie is an AAT student working for Klein LLB. Guthrie is currently working on the audit of Govan Ltd and has been told by his senior to 'hurry up and finish the audit as the budget is close to being exceeded'.

The senior also commented that Guthrie shouldn't worry about finding any more errors as 'the firm has a clause in its contract disclaiming liability, so is covered legally'.

Discuss the two comments made by the senior.

2 Tax services

2.1 Acceptance of tax clients

The key ethical issues relating to undertaking tax work are as follows:

- A member should not hold out to a client or an employer the assurance that any tax return prepared and tax advice offered are beyond challenge.

- A member should only undertake taxation work on the basis of full disclosure by the client or employer. The member, in dealing with the tax authorities, must act in good faith and exercise care in relation to facts or information presented on behalf of the client or employer.

2.2 Dealing with errors and omissions

In tax engagements it is likely that errors and omissions will be discovered. The ethical issue is how you deal with those errors and omissions. For example, a client might put an accountant under pressure not to disclose adjustments that would increase their tax liability. The relevant guidance is as follows:

A member should not be associated with any return or communication in which there is reason to believe that it:

- contains a false or misleading statement

- contains statements or information furnished recklessly or without any real knowledge of whether they are true or false or

- omits or obscures information required to be submitted and such omission or obscurity would mislead the tax authorities.

In the case of a member in practice, acting for a client, the member should furnish copies of all tax computations to the client before submitting them to HMRC.

When a member learns of a material error or omission in a tax return of a prior year, or of a failure to file a required tax return, the member has a responsibility to advise promptly the client or employer of the error or omission and recommend that disclosure be made to HMRC.

If the client or employer, after having had a reasonable time to reflect, does not correct the error, the member should inform the client or employer in writing that it is not possible for the member to act for them in connection with that return or other related information submitted to the authorities.

> Funds dishonestly retained after discovery of an error or omission become criminal property and their retention amounts to money laundering by the client or employer.

It is also a criminal offence in the UK for a person, including an accountant, to become concerned in an arrangement which he knows or suspects facilitates (by whatever means) the acquisition, retention, use or control of criminal property by or on behalf of another person.

A member in practice whose client refuses to make disclosure of an error or omission to HMRC, after having had notice of it and a reasonable time to reflect, is obliged to report the client's refusal and the facts surrounding it to the MLRO if the member is within a firm, or to the appropriate authority (NCA in the UK).

 Test your understanding 4

Saphira is an AAT member engaged in tax services and has discovered that one of her clients has omitted a material revenue item from the tax information they submitted to the tax office. Saphira has informed the company of the omission but has been told that it is their decision what they decide to submit and she should mind her own business.

What is the appropriate course of action?

3 Handling client monies

(Note: Handling client monies is not explicitly mentioned in the syllabus. It is included as background information for the professional accountant. It is linked in this respect to the wider business context and to assessment objective 1, 2 and 4.)

3.1 Introduction

Where accountants in practice hold client monies, such monies are held in trust and the accountant is acting as a trustee and must be prepared to account to the client upon request.

3.2 Handling client's monies

> **Definition**
>
> **Client monies** are any funds, or form of documents of title to money, or documents of title which can be converted into money that an accountant in practice holds on behalf of his or her client.
>
> This does not include any sum that is immediately due and payable on demand, for example the accountant in practice's fees for work done or fees paid in advance for work to be done.

Examples of items that will normally constitute client monies include:

- HMRC refunds received on behalf of clients
- Funds entrusted to an accountant in practice by the client to assist in carrying out the client's instructions
- Surplus funds that fall at the end of an engagement.

Note: Accountants in practice are prohibited from holding monies related to **investments** unless they are authorised to do so under the Financial Services and Markets Act 2000.

Client monies do not include the use and control of a client's own bank account. Where an accountant in practice has control of the client's own bank account, the client's specific written authority must have been obtained and acknowledged by the client's bank before the professional accountant in practice exercises any control over such bank account and adequate records of the transactions undertaken must be maintained.

3.3 Policy for handling monies belonging to others

Client monies cannot be held in certain circumstances, including:

- Where an accountant in practice knows or suspects the monies represent criminal property or are to be used for illegal activities.

- Where there is no justification for holding the monies, for example the monies do not relate to a service the accountant in practice provides.

- Where a condition on the accountant in practice's licence or registration prohibits dealing with client monies.

The following are conditions that apply when a Member in Practice holds client monies:

- The monies must be kept separately from personal monies or monies belonging to the practice.

- The monies must only be used for the purpose for which they were intended.

- The monies must be held in the same currency that it was received unless the client has given instructions to exchange into another currency.

- The accountant must ensure that the client has been identified and verified on a risk-sensitive basis before holding monies on their behalf.

- The accountant must be ready at all times to account for those monies or any income, dividends or gains generated on them, to the client or any persons entitled to such accounting.

 Test your understanding 5

Bobby is a professional accountant in practice.

One of Bobby's clients, Mr Corleone has asked her to hold £50,000 on his behalf, although he gives Bobby no explanation as to why she should take receipt of this money.

(a)   State whether you think Bobby should accept this request.

It transpires the money is needed to pay HMRC in six months' time, and Mr Corleone just wants to make sure the money is ring-fenced and available when needed.

(b)   (i)   What would you recommend Bobby should do with the money given this extra information?

(ii)   State TWO important procedures for handling clients' money.

(iii)   State which crime Bobby could be prosecuted for, if she decided to use the money for her own purposes?

---

4 Client confidentiality revisited

4.1 Confidentiality revisited

You will recall that in Chapter 1 we introduced the ethical principle of confidentiality, which essentially states that a member must respect the confidentiality of information acquired and not disclose any such information to third parties without proper and specific authority unless there is a legal or professional right or duty to disclose.

Since then we have seen situations where disclosure is not only permitted but may be required by law, such as in cases of suspected money laundering.

In this section we pull together and recap the key rules relating to confidentiality.

4.2 Circumstances when disclosure may be appropriate

Disclosure may be appropriate:

(a) where **permitted** by law and authorised by the client or the employer

(b) where **required** by law, for example:

    (i) provision of evidence in the course of legal proceedings or

    (ii) disclosure to the appropriate public authorities (for example, HMRC) of infringements of the law that come to light or

    (iii) disclosure of money laundering or terrorist financing.

(c) where there is a professional **duty** to disclose, which is in the public interest, and is not prohibited by law. Examples may include:

    (i) to comply with the quality review of an IFAC member body

    (ii) to respond to an inquiry or investigation by the AAT

    (iii) to protect the member's professional interests in legal proceedings

    (iv) to comply with technical standards and ethics requirements.

4.3 Deciding whether to disclose or not

In deciding whether to disclose confidential information, members should consider the following points:

(i)   whether the interests of all parties, including third parties, could be harmed by disclosure even though the client consents to the disclosure

(ii) whether all the relevant information is known and substantiated, to the extent that this is practicable

(iii) the type of communication or disclosure that may be made and by whom it is to be received; in particular, members should be satisfied that the parties to whom the communication is addressed are appropriate recipients.

 Test your understanding 6

Rory is a professional accountant working for JKLP, a large firm of accountants in practice. Rory qualified with a smaller firm but moved to JKLP two years ago.

Discuss the following matters from the point of view of confidentiality and whether or not disclosure should/could be made.

Matter 1

Client A is new to the practice and during routine tax work Rory has found a large understatement of tax in a prior year. The FD of client A is unwilling to tell HMRC about the error and has forbidden JKLP from doing so.

Matter 2

Recently one of the partners of JKLP started asking Rory for details about one of his old clients when he worked for the smaller firm.

Matter 3

Client B is looking to move premises and JKLP have been approached by the landlord asking for a reference concerning B's financial health.

Matter 4

Rory has just received a call from reception to tell him that two officers from the Fraud Squad are downstairs asking for information about one of JKLP's clients, Client C, to help in an investigation they are pursuing.

---

5 Other considerations

5.1 Fees

Fees should reflect the value of the professional services performed for the client, taking into account:

- the skill and knowledge required

- the level of training and experience required to perform the services

- the time required by each person engaged in performing the services, and

- the degree of responsibility that it entails.

It is not improper for a member to charge a client a lower fee than has previously been charged for similar services, provided the quality of the work does not suffer. However, members in public practice who obtain work at fees significantly lower than those charged by an existing accountant, or quoted by others, must be aware that there is a risk of a perception that the quality of work could be impaired.

Discounted audit fees are perceived as a 'self-interest' threat to professional behaviour. This does not mean that they should be avoided at all costs but guidelines need to be followed.

When a firm obtains an assurance engagement at a significantly lower fee level than that charged by the predecessor firm, or quoted by other firms, the self-interest threat created will not be reduced to an acceptable level **unless**

(i) the firm is able to demonstrate that appropriate time and qualified staff are assigned to the task, and

(ii) all applicable assurance standards, guidelines and quality control procedures are being complied with.

5.2 Publicity and advertising

Advertisements must comply with the local law and in the UK should conform as appropriate with the requirements of the British Code of Advertising Practice, and the ITC and Radio Authority Code of Advertising Standards and Practice, in particular as to legality, decency, clarity, honesty and truthfulness.

These considerations are of equal application to other promotional material, and to letterheads, invoices and similar practice documents.

If reference is made in promotional material to fees or the basis on which fees are calculated, the greatest care should be taken to ensure that such reference does not mislead as to:

- the precise services to be covered, and
- the basis of current and future fees.

Where members seek to make comparisons in their promotional material between their practices or services (including fees) and those of others, great care will be required. In particular, members should ensure that such comparisons:

- are objective and not misleading
- relate to the same services
- are factual and verifiable, and
- do not discredit or denigrate the practice or services of others.

Particular care is needed in relation to claims of size or quality. For example, it is impossible to know whether a claim to be 'the largest firm' in an area is a reference to the number of partners or staff, the number of offices or the amount of fee income. A claim to be 'the best firm' is subjective and incapable of substantiation, and should be avoided.

The advertisement itself should not, either in content or presentation, seek to promote services in such a way, or to such an extent, as to amount to harassment of a potential client. This is likely to deter the potential client and in the event of a complaint of harassment the burden of demonstrating that approaches of a repetitive and direct nature did not amount to harassment is likely to rest with the member.

5.3 Names and letterheads of practices

The name of a practice, which may feature on advertisements, letterheads, business cards and publications directed to clients or potential clients, must be consistent with the requirements of professional standing and with the dignity of the profession in the sense that it should not project an image inconsistent with that of a professional practice bound to high ethical and technical standards. It must comply with partnership and company law as appropriate, and, in the UK, with the Business Names Act 1985.

The name must be one that is not likely to:

- be misleading as to the nature or structure of the firm or the status of any person named in such letterhead or publicity. It should not, for instance, give an impression to the public that the firm is multi-partnered and broadly based when in fact it might be a very small firm. A practice with a limited number of offices should not describe itself as 'international' merely on the grounds that one of them is overseas

- bring the profession into disrepute; or

- be unfair to other practitioners or the public.

It should be clear from the letterhead of a practice whether any person named on it, other than persons named only in the name of the member firm, is a partner of the practice, a sole practitioner or a director.

 Test your understanding 7

GHYT is a firm of accountants in practice. The firm is currently running a new marketing campaign. The following are ideas that the partners want to include in the campaign.

Review the quotes given and decide whether they are appropriate or not. If not explain why.

- 'Are you being taken for a ride by your existing accountants?'

- 'We are the best and cheapest in our field'

- 'No hidden fees – the price you're given is the price you pay'

- 'Introduce a friend – get 10% off your fees'

- 'Our gift to you – your first personal tax return – half price'

6 Procedural aspects of new appointments

6.1 New clients

When a member is asked to provide accounting services or advice, he or she should enquire whether the prospective client has an existing accountant. There are three possible answers:

- The client has no existing accountant.

- There is an existing accountant who will continue to provide professional services.

- The client wants to change accountant.

6.2 Specific assignments with existing accountants

In cases where there is an existing accountant who will continue to provide professional services, the newly approached (receiving) accountant should limit the services provided to whatever specific assignment has been requested.

This will probably be an assignment of a type that is clearly distinct from that being carried out by the existing accountant and should be regarded as a separate request to provide services or advice.

Before accepting any appointments of this nature, the newly appointed accountant should communicate with the existing accountant and should do so immediately in writing, advising of the approach made by the client and the general nature of the request.

Where appropriate the existing accountant should maintain contact with the newly appointed accountants and co-operate with them in all reasonable requests for assistance.

Communication is meant to ensure that all relevant facts are known to the member who, having considered them, is then entitled to accept the nomination if he or she so wishes. However, care must be taken when communicating all relevant facts to a member in situations where the existing accountant knows or suspects that their client is involved in money laundering or a terrorist activity. Disclosure of money laundering or terrorist suspicion reporting to your potential successor should be avoided because this information may be discussed with your client or former client.

6.3 Replacing/changing accountants

Clients have the right to choose their professional advisers, and to change to others if they wish. There are many reasons why clients would wish to change accountants – it could be that:

- they are unhappy with the service

- they can get a better/cheaper service elsewhere

- their current supplier is closing their business

- the company has grown and the current accountant cannot cater for their expanded needs. Since it is impracticable for any one professional accountant in public practice to acquire special expertise or experience in all fields of accountancy some professional accountants in public practice have decided that it is neither appropriate nor desirable to develop within their firms the complete range of special skills that may be required.

While it is essential that the legitimate interests of the client be protected, it is also important that an accountant who is asked to replace another accountant has the opportunity to check if there are any professional reasons why the appointment should not be accepted.

The new accountant will, therefore, as a matter of professional ethics and routine, write to the previous accountant to request professional clearance and all relevant information and documents which will be required to fully take over the case.

The fact that there may be fees owing to the existing accountant is not a professional reason why another accountant should not accept the appointment. The existing accountant should promptly transfer to the new accountant all books and papers of the client which are or may be held after the change in appointment has been effected and should advise the client accordingly, unless the accountant has a legal right to withhold them.

After these procedural steps have been taken, the proposed successor should consider whether to accept the appointment or to decline it in the light of the information received from the existing adviser or from any other source, including any conclusions reached following discussion with the client.

6.4 Defamation

Under UK law an existing adviser who communicates to a potential successor matters damaging to the client or to any individuals concerned with the client's business will have a strong measure of protection were any action for defamation to be brought against him or her, in that the communication is likely to be protected by what is called 'qualified privilege'.

This means that the existing appointee should not be liable to pay damages for defamatory statements even if they should turn out to be untrue, provided that they are made without what the law regards as 'malice'.

There is little likelihood of an adviser being held to have acted 'maliciously' provided that:

- he or she states only what he or she sincerely believes to be true, and

- he or she avoids making reckless allegations against a client or connected individuals which he or she could have no reason for believing to be true.

Examples of statements that have been determined by the courts to be defamatory are those that involve; allegations of embezzlement, lying, irresponsibility, lack of integrity, dishonesty, laziness, incompetence, not being eligible for rehire, insubordination, being a traitor to the company, or having committed a criminal act.

 Test your understanding 8

Freddie Stott works for Jackman & Co. Freddie is helping a partner with a new tax client, Bridges Estate Management. Bridges is listed for an Inland Revenue Commissioners' meeting next Monday morning. Unfortunately, although Jackman & Co have made a professional enquiry and requested handover information from their predecessors (Allsorts Associates), no response has been received. This information is now needed urgently in order to help the new client at the Commissioners' meeting. Freddie has been asked to telephone Allsorts to demand the information.

Freddie called Amanda Florentini of Allsorts Associates on Thursday morning and explained the situation but even though told about the Inland Revenue Commissioners' meeting on Monday morning, she was not inclined to be helpful or release any information because Bridges still had not settled their account.

(a) Advise Freddie on whether his firm can begin to act for the client.

(b) Discuss whether or not Allsorts Associates should supply the handover information.

(c) Explain whether Freddie or his firm should try to get Bridges to pay their outstanding fees to Allsorts Associates.

(d) Until the situation is resolved, where else could Jackman & Co attempt to obtain the information?

7 Summary

We began this chapter by recapping the key principles that relate to accepting new work.

We recapped the principles of professional competence and objectivity and looked at some specific situations where these could be compromised.

We discussed particular issues relating to the handling of client monies, tax services and looked again at confidentiality – three key areas for the exam.

Next we looked other practical issues where ethical considerations are relevant. When obtaining professional work a member may promote and advertise the practice subject to guidance. The restrictions we outlined relate principally to the maintenance of professionalism. The Code of Professional Ethics sets out forms of unacceptable promotion e.g. use of coercion, material not in good taste, creating false or unjustified expectations, unfavourable comparisons with other members, etc.

Finally we covered some procedural aspects of public practice.

8 Test your understanding answers

Test your understanding 1

Professional competence and due care.

Test your understanding 2

Helen should inform the partners at Integrity LLP and should be removed from the audit of the client.

Test your understanding 3

First comment

It may be that Guthrie is working slower than expected, in which case the comment may be simply a harmless attempt at motivation.

However, the comment to hurry up the audit may mean that the job is not done to the correct standard, thus compromising the ethical principle of professional behaviour and due care.

If the senior puts pressure on Guthrie, then this could viewed as an intimidation threat to objectivity.

Second comment

Having professional indemnity insurance is no substitute for doing a professional job.

Test your understanding 4

Saphira should inform the MLRO of her firm.

A member in practice whose client refuses to make disclosure of an error or omission to HMRC, after having had notice of it and a reasonable time to reflect, is obliged to report the client's refusal and the facts surrounding it to the MLRO if the member is within a firm.

Test your understanding 5

(a) Bobby should refuse to accept the monies without further information. She needs to understand what the money is for to ensure that she is not being involved (unwittingly) in money laundering offences.

(b) (i) The £50,000 should be held separately in an interest bearing account.

(ii) Keep the money separate, use only for the purpose intended, be ready to account for the money at any time, pay any interest accrued into the clients account.

(iii) Theft or Fraud by abuse of position.

Test your understanding 6

Matter 1

A member in practice whose client refuses to make disclosure of an error or omission to HMRC, after having had notice of it and a reasonable time to reflect, is obliged to report the client's refusal and the facts surrounding it to the MLRO, who is then responsible for sending a SAR to NCA in the UK. This takes priority over client confidentiality.

Matter 2

An accountant is allowed to use general knowledge and experience from a previous employer but NOT specific information from that employer that is covered by the duty of confidentiality. Rory should respect confidentiality here and refuse to answer any questions for specific information regarding the prior client.

Matter 3

Writing the reference would be permitted only if Client C gave permission.

Matter 4

This is a complicated area of guidance that needs careful consideration before deciding how to proceed. The police do not have any automatic rights of access to JKLP's records but may hold a warrant or court order that would create a legal requirement for them to provide the information. Rory may want to get legal advice to establish the extent of the order and whether or not it could be challenged.

Test your understanding 7

- 'Are you being taken for a ride by your existing accountants?'

  Inappropriate – it calls the integrity of rival firms into question.

- 'We are the best and cheapest in our field.'

  Inappropriate – too non-specific – best and cheapest at what?

- 'No hidden fees – the price you're given is the price you pay.'

  Appropriate.

- 'Introduce a friend – get 10% off your fees.'

  Appropriate.

- 'Our gift to you – your first personal tax return – half price.'

  Appropriate.

 Test your understanding 8

(a) The firm can begin to act for Bridges on the basis of the verbal response to their professional enquiry. Jackman should, however, ensure that Allsorts Associates confirm their response in writing as soon as possible.

(b) Unless Allsorts can demonstrate that they have a particular right to retain the documents containing the information required by Jackman & Co, they should supply the information.

(c) Jackman & Co are under no obligation to intervene in any fee dispute. However, they may try to help if they feel able to do so.

(d) They might be able to obtain the information directly from Bridges or from HMRC.

9 Additional Test your understanding questions

Test your understanding 9

A trainee states that one of the main reasons she wanted to become an accountant is because she heard that if clients are happy with your work then they give you free gifts. Consider the following gifts and state the appropriate action in each case.

(a) A bottle of wine at Christmas.

(b) A free all expenses paid holiday.

Test your understanding 10

A new member of staff has offered to supply a list of clients from her old employer. He has also said that he has a lot of negative information about his old firm which he can tell you in order to help you gain clients from them.

Answer the following question by selecting the appropriate option.

In order to behave in an ethical way in these circumstances, which of the below is the most appropriate action to take?

A   Because he lacks integrity, this member of staff requires training in the form of CPD.

B   Because this person is disclosing confidential information, then they need reporting to the AAT.

C   Use the negative information in order to gain future clients.

Test your understanding 11

Your business partner wants to advertise in order to try and gain more clients. He has asked for your advice on the following points to include in an advert:

(a) He wants to imply that your practices and services are superior to those offered by other accountants.

(b) Your practice has three offices, one of which is on the Isle of Man, Your partner wishes to advertise the firm as 'Global.

(c) The phrases 'we can guarantee to reduce your tax bill' should be used in the advert.

10 Additional Test your understanding answers

Test your understanding 9

(a) A bottle of wine at Christmas.

Accept as this does not represent a significant financial sum.

(b) A free all expenses paid holiday.

Decline this offer as this is unreasonable and would impair objectivity.

Test your understanding 10

A

Because he lacks integrity, this member of staff requires training in the form of CPD.

Test your understanding 11

(a) Not appropriate – Care should be taken with comparisons as they should not discredit others.

(b) This is not appropriate as majority of the business is UK based and this would be misleading.

(c) This comment brings the profession into disrepute and should not be used.

Sustainability

6

Introduction

In this chapter we look at what is meant by sustainability and discuss what this means for the finance professional.

ASSESSMENT CRITERIA
1.1 Explain why it is important to act ethically
1.2 Explain how to act ethically
3.5 Explain the ethical responsibilities of accountants in upholding the principles of sustainability

CONTENTS
1 Sustainability
2 Triple Bottom Line (TBL) reporting
3 The role and responsibilities of the finance professional

1 Sustainability

1.1 What do we mean by 'sustainability'?

🔍 Definitions – Sustainability

There are a number of different definitions of sustainability:

- Sustainable development is development that meets the needs of the **present** without compromising the ability of **future** generations to meet their own needs.

  (The UN's Bruntland Report)

- A sustainable business is a business that offers products and services that fulfil society's needs while placing an equal emphasis on people, planet and profits.

  (The Sustainable Business Network)

- Sustainable trading is a trading system that does not harm the environment or deteriorate social conditions while promoting economic growth.

  (European Union (EU) website)

Sustainability can thus be thought of as an attempt to provide the best outcomes for the human and natural environments both now and into the indefinite future.

One aspect of this is the ability of the business to continue to exist and conduct operations with no effects on the environment that cannot be offset or made good in some other way.

Importantly, it refers to both the inputs and outputs of any organisational process.

- Inputs (resources) must only be consumed at a rate at which they can be reproduced, offset or in some other way not irreplaceably depleted.

- Outputs (such as waste and products) must not pollute the environment at a rate greater than can be cleared or offset.

Recycling is one way to reduce the net impact of product impact on the environment.

Firms should use strategies to neutralise these impacts by engaging in environmental practices that will replenish the used resources and eliminate harmful effects of pollution.

Example 1 – Firms acting sustainably

- Some logging companies plant a tree for every one they fell.

- Coca Cola is one of the companies that have taken a stand in writing a corporate water strategy where they aim to return as much water to nature and communities as they use in their drinks.

- Apple tries to make its products easy to recycle, helping to ensure that materials are reused rather than wasted.

However, it is important to note that sustainability is more than just looking at environmental concerns. It relates to environmental ('planet'), social ('people') and economic ('profit') aspects of human society.

 Example 2 – Unsustainable practices

Environmental

- deforestation

- the use of non-renewable resources including oil, gas and coal

- long term damage from carbon dioxide and other greenhouse gases.

Social

- anything contributing to social injustice

- rich consuming countries and poorer manufacturing countries

- rich companies exploiting third world labour as cheap manufacturing.

Economic

- strategies for short term gain (e.g. cutting staff costs to increase reported profits)

- paying bribes (also unethical and often illegal)

- underpayment of taxes.

 Test your understanding 1

Why do you think the under-payment of taxes (by large businesses in particular) is considered to be an unsustainable practice?

Test your understanding 2

Explain whether ongoing growth in air travel is sustainable in terms of the economic, environmental and social aspects of sustainability.

1.2   The risks of not acting sustainably

Sustainability affects every level of life, from the local neighbourhood to the entire planet. The main argument in favour of acting in a sustainable manner is that we have an ethical duty to do so. It is ethically wrong for this generation to benefit at the expense of future generations.

More specific examples of the problems of not acting ethically can be classified using the headings of economic, social and environmental risks.

 Example 3 – The risks of not acting sustainably

Environmental

- Deterioration of the environment and loss of some resources.
- Climate change – one of the greatest threats facing mankind.

Social

- Social sustainability encompasses human rights, labour rights, social justice and supporting the capacity of current and future generations to create healthy and liveable communities.
- Failure results in social injustice, infringement of human rights and a widening gap between the world's richest and poorest countries.

Economic

- There are limits to economic growth as the earth is a finite system.
- Only through sustainable development can a firm ensure long term growth.

1.3   Why businesses should act in a sustainable manner

Business sustainability is about ensuring that organisations implement strategies that contribute to long–term success.

Organisations that act in a sustainable manner not only help to maintain the well–being of the planet and people, they also create businesses that will survive and thrive in the long run.

In addition, it may be in the firm's **financial** interest to act sustainably.

Example 4 – How sustainability can boost profits

- Sustainability may help directly increase sales of products and services.

  For example, some customers may buy your product because a label on it says it has been manufactured using extra-safe working conditions for the labour force, or because it is Fair-trade.

- It may result in **cost savings**.

  For example, lower energy usage may reduce costs and increase profit.

- It may create **positive PR** and thus contribute to business in the long run.

  While sustainability may not enhance product sales right away, if it enhances the image of a company which in turn contributes to better business in the long-term, then it's worth it.

- Avoiding **fines** for pollution.

  The Deepwater Horizon oil spill in 2006 resulted in BP being fined $4.5 billion by the US Department of Justice. However, it is estimated that the total cost to date is in excess of $42 billion in terms of criminal and civil settlements and payments to a trust fund.

Directors have a duty to try to increase the wealth of their shareholders and some would see sustainability as conflicting with this objective.

However, many would argue that sustainability should result in better business performance in the long run.

Example 5 – Sustainability and business success

A recent working paper from Harvard Business School, '*The Impact Of A Corporate Culture Of Sustainability On Corporate Behaviour And Performance*', compared a sample of 180 US-based companies.

Over an 18-year period, those classified as high-sustainability companies dramatically outperformed the low-sustainability ones in terms of both stock market (i.e. share prices) and accounting measures (such as profit).

Example 6 – Holcim (Lanka) Ltd

Holcim (Lanka) Ltd, one of the leading suppliers of cement and aggregates in Sri Lanka, worked with local communities, focusing on communication and education, in combination with introducing more efficient waste management options.

As a result it has managed to

- create more profit ('profit')
- increase employment ('people') and
- reduce carbon emissions ('planet').

 Test your understanding 3

Suggest FOUR ways in which an airline could seek to limit its environmental footprint.

1.4 Sustainability and Corporate Social Responsibility (CSR)

Corporate social responsibility (CSR) refers to the idea that a company should be sensitive to the needs and wants of all its stakeholders, rather than just the shareholders.

It refers to an organisation's obligation to maximise its positive impacts upon stakeholders while minimising the negative effects.

A formal definition of CSR has been proposed by the World Business Council for Sustainable Development (WBCSD):

 Definition – CSR

'CSR is the continuing commitment by business to behave ethically and contribute to economic development while improving the quality of life of the workforce and their families as well as of the local community and society at large.'

(WBCSD meeting in The Netherlands, 1998)

KAPLAN PUBLISHING

Sustainability is thus one aspect of corporate social responsibility (CSR) and the two concepts are closely linked.

This is significant because many companies already have a commitment to CSR, setting targets and producing reports, for example. Calls to greater sustainability can thus be seen in the context of developing a firm's existing CSR policies and responsibilities, rather than something different and new.

2 Triple Bottom Line (TBL) reporting

2.1 Triple Bottom Line (TBL) reporting

A well-known saying in the world of business is 'what gets measured gets done'. If we want firms to change their behaviour with respect to sustainability, then there need to be systems in place that measure the economic, social and environmental impact of the firm's activities. Once these areas can be quantified in some way, then managers will take steps to improve their performance and incorporate such issues into future decisions.

A number of reporting frameworks have been developed to help in accounting for sustainability including the notion of triple-bottom-line (TBL) accounting.

TBL accounting expands the traditional company reporting framework to take into account environmental and social performance in addition to financial (economic) performance.

TBL thus attempts to show the full cost of any plans or development.

A key aspect of TBL is that it relates to both performance measurement and decision making. Once targets are set for these aspects and performance measured, then firms will incorporate the effects into decision making.

The concept is often explained using the triple 'P' headings of 'People, Planet and Profit'.

Example 7 – Triple Bottom Line Reporting

Planet

- A TBL company will try to reduce its 'ecological footprint' by managing resource consumption and energy usage and limiting environmental damage.

  For example, production processes will be efficient in terms of resource use and environmentally-damaging outputs such as toxic waste eliminated.

- The drive for environmental sustainability also means that TBL companies will not be involved in resource depletion.

  For example, fish stocks are maintained at sustainable levels and timber use is balanced by replanting to retain the resource into the future.

People

- A TBL business will ensure workers' rights are respected.

  For example, pay its workers fair wages, maintain a safe working environment and not use child labour.

- Similarly, the company would promote its surrounding community, for example by providing educational opportunities or a safe community to live in.

  For example, the Bourneville estate established by Cadbury the chocolate maker in England.

Profit

- A TBL company on will try to balance the profit objective with the other two elements of the TBL.

2.2 Problems with TBL

The first problem with TBL is that it can be difficult to measure the three factors concerned.

 Example 8 – Measuring performance using TBL

Typical measures include the following:

Planet

- Electricity consumption
- Fossil fuel consumption
- Water usage
- Amount of greenhouse gasses and other pollutants produced
- Percentage of resources recycled compared with dumped as landfill.

People

- Jobs created/unemployment rates
- Average pay levels
- Health and safety measures, such as accident rates
- Equality measures such as the diversity of employees.

Profit

- Profitability of individual businesses/divisions
- Taxes paid.

 Test your understanding 4

A UK company is looking at building a new factory in a third world country where there is currently high unemployment. Employees will work long hours with hazardous materials and the factory will produce levels of pollution that are legal in the country concerned but not in the UK. The company plans to build houses, schools and a health centre near the factory to look after employees.

Comment on the plan from a TBL perspective.

Test your understanding 5

The C Company manufactures a wide range of construction machinery such as diggers, tractors and large lorries. Each type of equipment is manufactured by one of seven different divisions, and each division is located in a major city, meaning that there are hundreds of kilometres between each division.

C also has an administration headquarters. This has been moved recently from an inner-city location to a new purpose built office building on an out-of-town site. The move has enabled C to provide extensive employee facilities including a sports complex and restaurant. Flexible working hours have also been introduced to allow employees to stagger their journey times; there is no public transport so all employees must travel in their own private cars.

The board of C are currently considering proposals for the use of the 'old' administration office site. The plan favoured by the finance director is the building of a waste disposal site as this has the highest return on investment. There is some disagreement over this move as the site is in a residential area although the local council has indicated agreement in principle to the proposal.

The finance director has also amended creditor payment terms from 30 to 60 days in order to improve C's cash flow situation. This move was part of a package of measures to improve cash flow. However, proposals to hold divisional meeting by videoconference rather than visiting each site, and carrying out an energy audit were vetoed by the board.

Discuss the sustainability performance of C Company by reference to the TBL headings of 'People, Planet and Profit'.

The second problem is that there are limits how far firms allow sustainability to impact decision making across the organisation.

 Example 9 – TBL in the banking industry

- Many banks claim to be committed to sustainability:

Planet

- They may have very energy-efficient buildings.

People

- Some banks give staff free days when they are paid to go out and engage in community assistance programmes.

- Others run 'managing your money' programmes, in which staff assists struggling families with financial planning and budgeting.

- Other activities include support programmes for hospitals, the Red Cross and schools.

Profit

- However, CIMA's research on the banking industry in New Zealand found **no evidence** that banks turn away profitable but less sustainable business in favour of sustainable but potentially less profitable business.

---

3 The role and responsibilities of the finance professional

Professional accountants have a responsibility to act in the public interest. This includes supporting sustainability and sustainable development and considering the risks to society as a whole of not acting sustainably.

3.1 Creating an ethics-based culture

As stated in Chapter 1, culture refers to the sum total of all the beliefs, attitudes, norms and customs that prevail within an organisation – 'the way we do things around here'. Ideally we want a culture that supports sustainability.

Finance professional can help in creating and promoting an ethics-based culture that discourages unethical or illegal practices, including money laundering, terrorist financing, fraud, theft, bribery, non-compliance with applicable regulations, bullying and short-term decision-making.

These issues have been covered in earlier chapters.

3.2 Championing sustainability

Rather than taking a reactive, passive approach to sustainability, finance professionals should take the initiative in raising awareness of social responsibility and the need to consider the impact of decisions and actions on sustainability. However, they need to remain objective while doing this.

This will involve promoting sustainable practices through the organisation in relation to the following:

Products and services

- Does making the product use inputs/materials/ingredients from renewable sources only?

- Does the firm source raw materials in ways that support their replenishment, safeguard natural habitats and ensure good animal welfare standards?

- What is the expected life of the product?

- How much of the product (including packaging) can be recycled?

- Is the level of packaging excessive?

Customers

- Does the firm have a recycling programme?

- What incentives are given to customers to encourage them to recycle?

- Does the firm encourage/help customers reduce their carbon footprint?

The supply chain

- Does the firm incorporate environmental considerations when selecting suppliers? For example, would it use a supplier with a poor record on pollution?

- Does the firm use suppliers who are geographically close to reduce the impact of transportation in terms of fuel used and exhaust emissions?

- Does the firm pay fair prices to suppliers or does it use its buying powers to drive prices down to very low levels?

- Does the firm encourage/help suppliers reduce their carbon footprint?

- Does the firm help suppliers reduce waste sent to landfill?

The workplace

- Does the firm have measurable targets for energy/water usage?
- Is the building energy efficient?

Employees

- Does the firm look after its employees in terms of working conditions, employment rights, job security, etc or are staff 'hired and fired' when necessary?
- Does the firm contribute to community projects?

Other business functions and processes

- Does the firm take into account environmental impacts of activities when making decisions?
- Does the firm measure the impact of social initiatives?

3.3 Risk management

Many finance professionals are involved in risk management as it is a key aspect of good corporate governance. For many firms this includes assessing risks such as the actions of competitors, the risk of machine breakdown, bad publicity, terrorist attacks and so.

However, this needs to be extended to include evaluating and quantifying reputational and other ethical risks.

In particular accountants can help highlight the risks of not acting sustainably.

3.4 Performance management

Performance management and decision making are areas that traditionally involve accountants and other finance professionals. As discussed above, accountants could encourage the firm to switch to 'triple bottom line reporting' or TBL.

Example 10 – Marks and Spencer

Marks and Spencer's 'Plan A' approach to sustainability and CSR is seen by many as an example of best practice in the retail industry and the company has received many industry and independent awards in this area.

Marks and Spencer has objectives in the following categories:

Climate change

- Help customers reduce carbon footprint
- Reduce operational greenhouse emissions
- Improve energy efficiency
- Help suppliers reduce their carbon footprint.

Waste

- Help customers reuse or recycle all products and packaging
- Reduce level of operational and construction waste sent to landfill
- Help suppliers reduce waste sent to landfill.

Natural resources

- Ensure efficient use of natural resources
- Source raw materials in ways that support their replenishment, safeguard natural habitats and ensure good animal welfare.

Being a fair partner

- Pay fair prices to suppliers
- Supporting local communities
- Ensuring good working conditions for everyone involved in the supply chains.

Health and wellbeing

- Improve health and nutritional benefits of products sold
- Influence diet and lifestyle choices, through clear nutritional labelling and information
- Encourage customers and employees to become more active.

Note: These are broken down into over 180 sub-objectives.

Test your understanding 6

Jadie works as a management accountant for a company that makes fish pies, fish fingers and breaded scampi for a major supermarket chain. The company's marketing includes a statement that all fish is obtained from renewable sources.

Recently Jadie came across a supplier's invoice for monkfish, a species identified by Greenpeace as being under particular pressure from fishing.

Comment on the situation, firstly from a sustainability perspective and secondly from an ethical perspective. What should Jadie do?

4 Summary

A key to understanding sustainability is to consider the UN Bruntland Report definition – we (the present generation) must not compromise future generations in the pursuit of our own objectives and plans.

In particular we need to incorporate social, economic and environmental considerations (also known as people, profit and planet) into performance management and decision making. One way of doing this is via Triple Bottom Line Reporting.

The finance professional can contribute towards this by creating an ethics-based culture, championing sustainability, incorporating it into risk management and by ensuring sustainability features in performance management and decision making.

5 Test your understanding answers

 ## Test your understanding 1

Underpayment of tax is considered to be unsustainable as the organisations concerned are not contributing to maintaining the country's infrastructure (schools, roads, etc.).

 ## Test your understanding 2

Economic sustainability

- In the short term airline companies are stable due to demand for air travel.

- In the long term airline companies may not be sustainable as air travel in its current form cannot be provided indefinitely.

- There are limits to growth as air travel currently depends on the use of non-renewable resources (primarily oil).

Environmental sustainability

- Air travel does not appear to be sustainable due to damage to the environment (carbon dioxide emissions).

- As noted above, air travel also uses non-renewable resources.

- Damage to the environment may continue, as long term effects, such as global warming, take longer to be noticed.

Social sustainability

- It could be argued that air travel has a positive social benefit because it can change communities by providing cheap and quick methods of moving people around the world.

- Individual communities find it more difficult to be 'isolated' or unchanged by other social systems.

- However, while appearing 'cheap', air travel is still expensive for poorer communities. In social terms it accentuates the difference between richer countries (where 'cheap' air travel is affordable) and poorer countries (where air travel is still 'expensive').

Test your understanding 3

- Discuss more efficient aircraft and engine design with manufacturers. For example the new Airbus A350 claims to reduce fuel consumption by 25% over similar sized aircraft.

- Provide information to customers on the environmental impact of air travel. Some may choose to use alternative methods of transportation or use a carbon offsetting scheme.

- Limit the amount of baggage customers are allowed to carry – and impose surcharges for amounts over this limit. This will reduce fuel consumed and greenhouse gases produced.

 Test your understanding 4

Planet

- The level of pollution is worrying. Of particular concern is the fact that this would not be legal in the UK indicating that even if the pollution is legal in the country concerned the level is ethically wrong.

- Furthermore there is no evidence that the firm is planning any clean up or off-setting activities.

People

- Working conditions would be considered unethical and unsustainable.

- However, in defence of the firm they are contributing to the local community via wages, job creation, housing, schools and a health centre.

Profit

- Despite the social initiatives described above, it is difficult not to conclude that the firm is building the factory in the country concerned primarily to save costs and avoid UK legislation regarding employment and environmental standards.

Test your understanding 5

People

The C Company appears to be meeting this objective for its own staff. The provision of flexible working hours, staff restaurant and sports facilities all indicate a caring, sustainable attitude towards staff.

However, the ability of C Company to take into account other stakeholder interests is unclear. Specific areas of concern include the following.

- Delaying payment for raw materials will adversely affect the cash flow of C's suppliers. This could compromise their (i.e. the supplier's) long term survival.

- Moving the administration headquarters 'out of town' does not necessarily help the community. For example, there will be increased pollution as C's employees drive out to the administration building (note that there is no public transport).

- While flexible working time is allowed, this may mean travel time has increased. This may place pressure on workers regarding collection of children on 'school runs' and mean more cars on the road increasing the risk of accidents. Provision of company buses out to the new headquarters would help decrease pollution but would not necessarily assist with the working hours issue.

- The proposal for the redevelopment of the old administration headquarters into a waste disposal centre is unlikely to benefit the community. There will be additional heavy lorries travelling through residential areas while the burning of rubbish provides the risk of fumes and smoke blowing over residential properties. Finding an alternative use, even if this was less profitable, would benefit the community overall.

Planet

Areas of concern include the following.

- Lack of an energy audit. A review of energy consumption could identify areas for energy saving, even if this was only the use of low wattage light bulbs.

- The relocation of the administration office to an out-of-town area may enhance working conditions for staff, but it also means that public transport cannot be used to reach the offices. This increases fuel use as employees must use their own transport.

- The insistence of the chairman in holding all divisional review meetings in person rather than using newer technology such as videoconferencing means increased use of air travel and therefore carbon dioxide emissions.

Profit

At present, the C Company appears to be placing a lot of importance on the profit motive. Two specific decisions to increase profits are:

- delaying payment to creditors to provide additional cash within C and therefore decreasing the need for bank overdrafts, which in turn decreases interest payments.

- the proposal for the redevelopment of the old administration headquarters into a waste disposal site, which appears to be focused entirely on the amount of profit that can be made.

 Test your understanding 6

- From a sustainability perspective the use of monkfish should be discouraged as (1) overfishing could result in it no longer being a feasible food source – i.e. the fishing is unsustainable – and (2) overfishing could result in the species becoming extinct.

- In addition, from an ethical perspective, it is wrong for the company to mislead customers with its claims that all fish are from renewable sources if, in fact, that is not the case.

- In the first instance Jadie should try to gather more information. It may be that this particular monkfish is sourced from a fish farm and hence sustainable, or that the invoice was wrong or the supplier sent the wrong fish and the company wouldn't knowingly use it or that the Greenpeace advice is not considered authoritative or some other reasonable explanation.

- If she is still concerned, then she should discuss the matter with her manager and/or the head of purchasing.

6 Additional Test your understanding questions

Test your understanding 7

Vincent is a recently qualified accountant working at Biggs Engineering plc. At the last management meeting the Finance Director stated that the firm needed to take sustainability more seriously as it seemed to be becoming more important in negotiations to win new customers.
A recent incident involving the dumping of toxic chemicals lost Biggs Engineering a major client.

The FD mentioned the Bruntland Report and a possible move to Triple Bottom Line reporting and Vincent was given the job of explaining these ideas to other staff members.

Required:

(a) What are the two main features of the UN Bruntland Report definition of sustainability?

(b) As an accountant, does Vincent have any responsibilities with respect to sustainability?

(c) What is meant by Triple Bottom Line reporting?

(d) What steps can Vincent take to move the firm forwards in terms of sustainability?

Test your understanding 8

Which of the following might raise ethical issues for a manufacturer of chocolate?

(i) The materials used in the production of the chocolate.

(ii) The quality of the chocolate.

(iii) How the chocolate is advertised.

(iv) How much its cocoa supplier pays its staff.

(v) How much it pays its own staff.

Test your understanding 9

HGF Ltd is considering implementing a corporate social responsibility (CSR) policy to improve its sustainability record. However it is concerned that there may be drawbacks to this.

An employee has identified a list of possible problems caused by a CSR policy.

(1)　Increased materials cost

(2)　Failure to attract and retain quality employees

(3)　Loss of management time

(4)　Loss of key business skills

Which of these are valid concerns?

7 Additional Test your understanding answers

 Test your understanding 7

(a) The two main aspects of the Bruntland Report definition are that sustainable development is development that (1) meets the needs of the present (2) without compromising the ability of future generations to meet their own needs.

(b) Professional accountants have a responsibility to act in the public interest. This includes supporting sustainability and sustainable development and considering the risks to society as a whole of not acting sustainably.

(c) TBL accounting expands the traditional company reporting framework to take into account environmental and social performance in addition to financial (economic) performance.

(d) Vincent can move the firm forwards in terms of sustainability by the following:

Creating an ethics-based culture

Ideally we want a culture that supports sustainability and discourages unethical or illegal practices, including

Championing and promoting sustainability

Vincent can help promote sustainable practices in relation to products and services, customers, employees, the workplace, the supply chain and business functions and processes.

Risk management

Vincent can help highlight the risks of not acting sustainably and draw attention to reputational and other ethical risks.

Performance management

Vincent can help introduce TBL – see above.

Test your understanding 8

All of the issues mentioned would raise ethical issues.

Materials used impacts on the safety of the product. Quality is a safety issue. Advertising raises issues of truth and manipulation. The treatment and potential exploitation of labour, whether directly employed by a business or its suppliers, is also an ethical issue.

Test your understanding 9

(1) and (3) are valid concerns but (2) and (4) are incorrect.

CSR is likely to attract good quality employees and should not lead to a loss of key skills within the organisation.

However, goods need to be purchased from ethical sources, which may lead to a rise in their cost. It can also take up significant amounts of management time, which could have been used to increase business profits.

PRACTICE ASSESSMENT

1 Practice Assessment Questions

THE FOLLOWING MOCK IS A <u>PRACTICE EXAM</u> ONLY AND IS NOT PRESENTED IN REAL EXAM STYLE.

INSTRUCTIONS TO CANDIDATES

To 'state' something, you need to answer with a fact. If you are asked to 'explain' something you need to state the relevant fact and then give brief reason(s) for why that fact is the right answer. If you are asked to 'describe' you should set out what is involved without further explanation.

The time allowed to complete this Ethics for Accountants assessment is 2 hours and 30 minutes.

Task 1

(8 marks)

(a) Which body is responsible for regulating the UK accountancy profession as a whole?

(b) Which body sets global ethical standards for accountants?

(c) State TWO of the four sponsoring bodies of AAT.

(d) State TWO of the three statutory regulated (reserved) areas in accountancy and finance.

(e) All professional accountants have five ethical principles which they have a duty to comply with. Explain whether this duty is more important for professional accountants in practice rather than those in business.

Task 2

(12 marks)

(a) Professional accountants are required to undertake continuing professional development (CPD).

State which ONE of the five fundamental principles is safeguarded by CPD.

(b) Charis is a professional accountant with her own small practice. She prepares sets of accounts and tax returns for a wide range of sole traders.

In light of her client base, explain ONE area of technical knowledge in which Charis must keep up-to-date.

(c) **Complete the following statement:**

'A professional accountant who complies with the law, brings no disrepute on the profession and is perceived as being ethical by other people has complied with the fundamental principle of...'

(d) Frank, a professional accountant in practice, has acted outside the limits of his professional expertise in working for his client Nancy. Nancy has incurred a regulatory fine as a result.

State TWO grounds on which Nancy may be able to seek compensation from Frank for this loss.

(e) Christie is a professional accountant in practice who has had Alpha Ltd as a client for many years. In her professional capacity, Christie has been asked by Alpha Ltd's new landlord to give a written reference confirming that the company is likely to be able to pay rent over the next five years. Alpha Ltd is paying Christie a large fee for supplying the reference.

(i) **Is it acceptable practice for Christie to include a disclaimer of liability in the written reference?**

(ii) **If Christie gives the reference, even though she knows that Alpha Ltd has no means of paying the rent, what kind of fraud is she committing?**

(f) Marion, a professional accountant in practice, gives Larch Ltd an opinion on the application of accounting principles to the company's specific transactions. Marion knew that she was forming her opinion on the basis of inadequate information.

In addition to integrity, state which other ONE of Marion's fundamental ethical principles is threatened by this situation.

Explain the reasons for your answer.

(g) Henry is a professional accountant. He finished his exams and qualified a year ago.

State ONE way in which Henry can ensure he keeps up-to-date with technical changes in accounting and reporting.

Task 3 (5 marks)

Leonardo is a professional accountant in practice as a sole practitioner. His client, Alana, has given Leonardo £10,000 to hold on her behalf so that he can transfer money for her to HM Revenue and Customs (HMRC) when necessary. Leonardo now has good reason to believe the money is criminal property.

(a) With what crime could Leonardo be charged if he retains Alana's money without notifying the authorities?

(b) Leonardo has taken custody of monies for another client so that he can carry out the client's instructions.

    (i) In what legal capacity does Leonardo hold these client monies for the client?

    (ii) For what TWO crimes could Leonardo be prosecuted if he fails to properly account to the client for the monies?

    (iii) May Leonardo retain these monies in his practice bank account?

Task 4 (5 marks)

(a) Professional accountants must maintain the confidentiality of information which is obtained in circumstances that give rise to a duty of confidentiality.

    Is this an ethical principle only, a legal obligation only, or both an ethical principle and a legal obligation?

(b) **Explain whether a professional accountant is allowed to use knowledge, information and experience gained from a previous employer in a new job.**

(c) George is a professional accountant in practice. He has several pieces of confidential information about his client Mabel.

    State whether it may be appropriate for George to disclose the information in the following circumstances:

    (i) Disclosure to the appropriate public authority of Mabel's infringement of the criminal law.

    (ii) Disclosure which is not required by law but which is authorised by Mabel.

Tasks 5 – 9

Tasks 5 – 9 are based on the following project scenario and the six matters listed. Each task indicates which of the six specific matters is/are relevant to the task.

Project scenario

ABC Co is a well-established firm of accountants with a single office in the city of Standley. In total ABC Co employs ten fully qualified professional accountants, three part-qualified student accountants and six administrative staff.

Any letters received in the post by ABC Co are opened immediately by one of the administrative staff. They are then left in a closed folder on the relevant person's desk.

ABC Co's clients include:

- Straithard Ltd, a trading company run by Mick Gurdy

- Williams Ltd, a small painting and decorating company with annual revenue of £50,000 and annual profits of £10,000

- Crawthorne Ltd, a company which manufactures high quality wooden furniture to order

- Unwin Ltd and Idris Ltd, both of which are technology companies based in Standley.

Bradley Ltd, a new client operating in the transport sector.

You are Chris, one of the three part-qualified student accountants at ABC Co. You report to Ian, one of the fully qualified professional accountants.

Recently the following six matters have come to light.

Matter 1

Eliza Brown, one of the fully qualified professional accountants in ABC Co, has been off sick for a week. Your line manager Ian asked you to go through the mail folder on Eliza's desk to see if there was anything that needed to be dealt with urgently. You found the following note:

Note from: Mick Gurdy, Straithard Ltd

Addressed to: Eliza Brown, ABC Co.

> Eliza
>
> I'm pretty disappointed that you haven't answered my emails or texts. I thought I had made it clear to you that I'll let you have that £500 you need for your holiday but only if you go ahead and include on the company's tax return the revenue figure that I gave you. I don't care that it's much less than the figure from the accounts. You know that if you don't do as I say by the end of the month I'm going to tell your firm about the other ways in which you have helped me manipulate our figures in the past. This is your last chance.
>
> Mick

Matter 2

Williams Ltd, a small painting and decorating company, has unexpectedly requested ABC Co help it to apply for a gambling licence and to look for premises for a casino costing £10 million.

Matter 3

In response to best-practice guidelines issued by its trade organisation and encouragement from ABC Co, Crawthorne Ltd has drafted a six-point Code of Practice for use within the company's finance function. You have been handed the following extract:

> *Confidential*
>
> Extract from draft Code of Practice for finance function of Crawthorne Ltd
>
> For reference only by Crawthorne Ltd's finance function staff in the course of their duties
>
> Drafted by: Kenny Long, Assistant Accountant, Crawthorne Ltd
>
> Each member of Crawthorne Ltd's finance function staff will ensure that:
>
> 1   Any request for information from regulators, staff, customers or suppliers will be treated in a timely manner and with openness, honesty, accuracy and respect.
>
> 2   Personal information held in the finance function will be treated with respect and in line with relevant statutory requirements.
>
> 3   Purchase prices paid to suppliers for goods and services will be reviewed by a senior person in terms of their fairness to both parties if a complaint is raised by the supplier.

4   Payments to all suppliers will be made so that funds are received by them no later than 30 days after the relevant invoice has been recorded, unless some other arrangement has been expressly agreed with the supplier.

5   No individual finance function member will accept an offer of a gift or hospitality from any person unless (a) it's worth is less than £20 AND (b) the same offer is made to all or substantially all of the person's business associates.

6   Any complaint from Crawthorne Ltd employees about the amount or timing of a payroll payment will be reviewed and responded to within 24 hours of its receipt in the finance function.

When looking at the company's file you also note that Crawthorne Ltd recently asked ABC Co for advice in relation to an e-mail received from one of its customers, Tolly Ltd. Tolly Ltd had ordered furniture to a value of £200 from Crawthorne Ltd.

From: r.askew@tollyltd.com

To: k.long@crawthorneltd.co.uk

Subject: Payment error

Hi Kenny

Stupidly we have made a transfer of funds to you in error, even though you have not yet delivered the furniture to us. Our transfer is for £20,000. It would be embarrassing to have the money repaid to our bank account so could you transfer £19,800 instead to the bank account of: Japes Ltd, sort code 30-25-94, account number 98924983? You can keep hold of £200 in advance payment of your invoice to us once raised.

Ryan Askew, Tolly Ltd

You note that on the advice of ABC Co, Crawthorne Ltd did not make the requested transfer because of the possibility of this action implicating Crawthorne Ltd in illegal activity by Tolly Ltd. The matter is still being investigated.

Matter 4

For several years Bernard, one of ABC Co's fully qualified professional accountants, has dealt with two competing technology companies, Unwin Ltd and Idris Ltd. The two companies have existing premises in Standley Science Park, where a new building has just been completed. Idris Ltd and Unwin Ltd are both putting in a bid to lease the whole of the new building. They each asked Bernard to act for them in relation to the bid. When the companies realised they were both interested in leasing the same building, Idris Ltd offered Bernard an extra £3,000 to act for it exclusively; Unwin Ltd also offered Bernard an additional £3,000 for exclusive representation. Neither company is willing for Bernard to act for both parties with respect to the lease.

Matter 5

Very recently ABC Co started an engagement for a new client operating in the transport sector, Bradley Ltd, following appropriate customer due diligence procedures. Sam, one of ABC Co's fully qualified professional accountants, had been working on Bradley Ltd's accounts for a short time when she realised that a serious tax error had been made in the previous period's tax return. The tax error was made by Bradley Ltd's financial controller, Vince, and led to a large underpayment of tax. Sam has brought this error to Vince's attention but the directors of Bradley Ltd categorically refuse to disclose the error to HMRC. Sam needs to decide firstly whether ABC Co should continue to act for Bradley Ltd and secondly whether she has any external reporting requirements in respect of Bradley Ltd.

Matter 6

One of ABC Co's newest fully qualified professional accountants, Jamie, is very keen to promote sustainability and sustainable development in the firm, and has made a presentation to the firm's staff which mentions

- the Brundtland definition of sustainability

- that professional accountants are obliged to support sustainability as far as they are able in the context of their work

- that ABC Co should champion sustainability by encouraging its clients to focus on their 'triple bottom line'.

Unfortunately no-one is clear about what Jamie actually meant.

Task 5 (10 marks)

Refer to the Project Scenario and Matter 1.

(a) **Explain which THREE of Eliza Brown's fundamental principles are most threatened by the situation outlined in Mick Gurdy's note.**

(b) **In terms of the conceptual framework, explain the TWO threats being faced by Eliza.**

Task 6 (10 marks)

Refer to the Project Scenario and Matters 2 and 3.

(a) **Explain whether ABC Co should conduct customer due diligence (CDD) procedures with respect to Williams Ltd's request about the gambling licence and casino.**

(b) **Explain THREE of Crawthorne Ltd's key ethical organisational values with reference to its draft Code of Practice.**

(c) **Explain whether Crawthorne Ltd's Code of Practice will be a statutory code once it is implemented.**

Task 7 (10 marks)

Refer to the Project Scenario and Matter 4.

(a) **Explain which TWO of Bernard's fundamental principles are threatened by the fact that both Idris Ltd and Unwin Ltd are bidding for the lease on the same building in Standley Science Park.**

(b) **Describe the ethical conflict resolution process that Bernard should undertake in deciding how to act in respect of this matter. Assume that he will be able to resolve the conflict of interest without external professional advice.**

(c) **Assuming he decides he can act for one of the clients, explain TWO issues Bernard must consider when carrying out the engagement.**

Task 8 (10 marks)

Refer to the Project Scenario and Matter 5.

(a) (i) Explain the actions Sam must take in respect of Bradley Ltd.

   (ii) Explain the consequences for Sam if the actions in (a) (i) are NOT taken.

(b) Explain what actions Vince should take about Bradley Ltd's refusal to report to HMRC, and what protection these actions will give him.

Task 9 (10 marks)

Refer to the Project Scenario and Matter 6.

(a) Explain the TWO key aspects of sustainability as set out in the UN Brundtland Report.

(b) Explain the nature of the professional accountant's obligation to uphold the values of sustainability.

(c) Explain what Jamie meant by 'the triple bottom line' for ABC Co's clients.

(d) Describe for your accountant colleagues in ABC Co FOUR ways in which they can seek to support sustainability and sustainable development within ABC Co itself.

2 Practice Assessment Answers

Task 1 (8 marks)

(a) The Financial Reporting Council (FRC).

(1 mark) LO1.2

(b) International Ethics Standards Board for Accountants (IESBA) or International Federation of Accountants (IFAC).

(1 mark for any one of these) LO1.3

(c) Any two of the following: ICAEW, CIMA, CIPFA or ICAS.

(1 mark each, max 2) LO1.3

(d) Any two of the following: Audit, investment business or insolvency.

(1 mark each, max 2) LO1.2

(e) It is EQUALLY important for accountants in business to comply as for those in practice, because these are the fundamental principles of the profession even if how they are complied with is different.

(1 mark for EQUALLY or equivalent; 1 mark for explanation EITHER as to principle *being fundamental or equivalent, OR that how they comply is different because of circumstances but the duty to comply is the same) LO1.2*

Task 2 (12 marks)

(a) Professional competence and due care.

(1 mark; can accept just 'professional competence') LO1.6

(b) Identify one of: regulation of accounting; tax legislation/compliance; money laundering regulation; accounting/reporting standards.

(1 mark; NO marks for auditing, companies legislation, regulation of the profession, changes in other areas of criminal law, changes in ethical codes as irrelevant to scenario/not the MOST important areas).

Reason given for importance of area selected for sole traders because clients are businesses which must comply with requirement for accurate accounts preparation and tax returns/Charis needs to protect herself re money laundering.

(1 mark for explanation) LO1.6

(c)   Professional behaviour.

(1 mark) LO2.1

(d)   An action for breach of contract. An action for professional negligence.

(1 mark for breach of contract, 1 mark for negligence) LO2.6

(e)   (i)   Yes

(1 mark) LO2.6

     (ii)   Fraud by false representation.

(1 mark) LO2.6

(f)   Professional competence and due care.

(1 mark; award ½ mark if only competence or due care).

Marion is not acting diligently nor is she in accordance with applicable professional standards by giving an opinion without having access to adequate information.

(1 mark for diligence or equivalent, 1 mark for applicable professional standards or equivalent). LO3.2

(g)   Read professional journals; attend technical update courses; comply with CPD requirements.

(1 mark only for ONE answer that is specific and relevant; NO marks for generic answer like 'read the newspapers, listen to business programmes on the radio, pay his membership fees' etc.) LO1.6

Task 3 (5 marks)

(a)   Money laundering.

(1 mark; NO marks for fraud, theft, tipping off, failure to disclose or prejudicing an investigation) LO2.4

(b)   (i)   In trust/as a trustee

(1 mark for either) LO2.4

     (ii)   Theft, fraud by abuse of position

(1 mark each, max 2 marks) LO2.4

     (iii)   No.

(1 mark) LO2.4

Task 4 **(5 marks)**

(a) BOTH an ethical principle and a legal obligation.

(1 mark) LO2.5

(b) An accountant is allowed to use general knowledge and experience from a previous employer *(1 mark)* but NOT specific information from that employer that is covered by the duty of confidentiality.

(1 mark). LO2.5

(c) (i) Yes, may be appropriate to disclose

(1 mark) LO2.5

(ii) Yes, may be appropriate to disclose.

(1 mark) LO2.5

Task 5 **(10 marks)**

(a) The THREE fundamental principles most threatened are:

- Integrity: including false figures is being associated with misleading information, and it is dishonest.

  (Integrity 1 mark; explanation 1 mark) LO1.1

- Objectivity: giving in to threats/pressure/the offer of payment is allowing a conflict of interest/undue influence to override or compromise professional judgement.

  (Objectivity 1 mark; explanation 1 mark) LO1.1

- Professional behaviour: submitting false figures to HMRC is in breach of relevant laws and regulations and brings the accounting profession into disrepute.

  (Professional behaviour 1 mark; explanation 1 mark) LO1.1

(Do NOT accept confidentiality, or professional competence and due care)

(b) • Self-interest threat from Mick's offer of £500 for her holiday.

  (1 mark self-interest; 1 mark for identifying the offer of £500 for her holiday as the explanation). LO2.1

- Intimidation threat from Mick's statement that he will report her past behaviour to her firm.

  (1 mark for intimidation; 1 mark for identifying Mick's statement that he will reveal her behaviour as the explanation). LO2.1

Task 6 (10 marks)

(a)   Yes, ABC Co should conduct CDD *(1 mark)* as these suggested transactions appear to be inconsistent with prior knowledge of the client and the client's normal business which is painting and decorating on a small scale.

(1 mark for explanation). LO1.5

(b)   Three from the following:

- Reporting financial and regulatory information clearly and on time (refer to point 1)

- Being transparent with colleagues, customers and suppliers (refer to point 1)

- Being open and honest by identifying when it is appropriate to accept gifts and hospitality (refer to point 5)

- Paying suppliers a fair price and on time (refer to points 3 and 4)

- Providing fair treatment to employees (refer to points 2 and 6).

(1 mark each for any of the following key values with explanation that implicitly or explicitly refers to Crawthorne's Code, max 3 marks) LO1.4, LO2.3

(c)   No, it will not be statutory.

(1 mark for not statutory).

The code has been created in response only to the trade organisation's best practice guidelines and ABC Co's encouragement, so it is clearly a voluntary one prepared by Crawthorne Ltd for its own use / The code cannot be statutory since that would be created under legislation / regulation / case law and used by many companies.

(1 mark for explanation: EITHER it is not created by legislation etc OR it is only created for one company OR it is voluntary in response to trade body/ABC Co best practice guidelines). LO1.4, LO2.3

(d) 'Point 7: Finance function staff will remain vigilant to the risks of being unwittingly involved in money laundering, bribery and other illegal acts.

In particular, any overpayment by a customer will be thoroughly investigated by a senior member of finance function staff and only repaid to the customer once it has been established that it is right/legal to do so.'

(1 mark for vigilant or equivalent, 1 mark for money laundering OR bribery OR fraud OR any other relevant illegal acts, 1 mark for reference to/appropriate response to similar situation to Tolly Ltd). LO1.5

Task 7
(10 marks)

(a) Objectivity – because it is difficult to act without a perception of bias when the two clients' interests are in such conflict because they both want the lease; and Confidentiality – because he has confidential information in respect of each client.

(1 mark for objectivity and 1 mark for explanation; 1 mark for confidentiality and 1 mark for explanation). LO2.2, LO3.5

(b) Bernard should:

- consider relevant facts/ethical issues involved/his fundamental principles/any established procedures in ABC Co

  (1 mark for WHAT he should consider); LO3.5

- establish alternative courses of action, establish which is most consistent with the fundamental principles and establish the consequences of each

  (1 mark for: establishing alternative courses of action; establishing consistency with principles; consequences of alternatives, MAX 2 marks); LO3.5

- seek advice about the matter within ABC Co, and document the substance of the issue and discussions.

  (1 mark for EITHER seeking internal advice OR documenting conflict resolution process). LO3.5

(c) In acting for one of the clients Bernard should consider instituting appropriate safeguards so that his familiarity with the other client does not affect his professional judgement/objectivity, and so that he does not breach confidentiality re the other party.

(1 mark for safeguard for objectivity, 1 mark for safeguard for confidentiality). LO2.2, LO3.5

Task 8   **(10 marks)**

(a) (i)   Sam must inform Bradley Ltd that she/ABC Co can no longer
            act for Bradley Ltd *(1 mark)* because funds dishonestly retained
            after discovery of a tax error become criminal property so their
            retention amounts to money laundering by Bradley Ltd.
            (1 mark). Sam must make an internal report on the matter to
            ABC Co's MLRO.

            (1 mark for internal report to MLRO (NOT SAR or NCA)).
            LO3.1, LO3.3

     (ii) If Sam further facilitates Bradley Ltd's retention of the funds
            related to the tax error by continuing to act for it, Sam will
            herself be engaged in money laundering. *(1 mark)*. As ABC Co
            is a firm in the regulated sector, if the action required under the
            Proceeds of Crime Act is not taken then Sam will have
            committed the crime of failure to disclose.

            *(1 mark for regulated sector or equivalent, 1 mark for failure to
            disclose). LO3.3*

(b) As he is now aware of the error, Vince should report to NCA that he
     suspects Bradley Ltd of money laundering because it has refused to
     notify the matter to HMRC. *(1 mark for advice to make a report to
     NCA)*. He will be protected from a claim for breach of confidentiality
     when making this report. *(1 mark)*. Knowing he may have been
     involved in money laundering, Vince needs to make an authorised
     disclosure to NCA *(1 mark for authorised disclosure to NCA)* which
     may help protect him from a charge that he himself, in making the
     error, was engaged in money laundering.

     (1 mark for its protective effect). LO3.4

Task 9 (10 marks)

(a)   'Meeting the needs of the present without compromising the ability of future generations to meet their own needs'.

(1 mark for 'meeting the needs of the present' or equivalent, 1 mark for 'without compromising future generations' or equivalent). LO4.2

(b)   Obligation is part of professional accountant's responsibility to act in the public interest. This includes supporting sustainability and sustainable development and considering the risks to society as a whole of not acting sustainably.

(1 mark for 'public interest', 1 mark for element of explanation). LO2.3, LO4.1

(c)   Taking social, environmental and financial factors into account when measuring position and performance for clients or when assisting with their decision-making.

(½ mark for 'social'; ½ mark for 'environmental'; ½ mark for 'financial'; ½ mark for EITHER context of performance measurement OR assisting with decision-making). LO4.2

(d)   Any four from the following:

- promote sustainable practices through ABC Co re services, clients, fellow employees, the workplace, the supply chain and business functions/processes

- encourage long-term responsible management/use of resources within ABC Co

- facilitate ABC Co being run in a sustainable manner

- highlight within ABC Co the risks of not acting sustainably

- take social/environmental/ethical factors into account when assisting with decision-making or performance/position measurement.

(1 mark for each valid separate point, max 4 marks) (detail not needed for mark to be awarded) LO4.2

INDEX

KAPLAN PUBLISHING